PENGUIN BOOKS

ON DEATH

Timothy Keller started Redeemer Presbyterian Church in New York City with his wife, Kathy, and their three sons. Redeemer grew to nearly 5,500 regular Sunday attendees and helped to start more than three hundred new churches around the world. In 2017 Keller moved from his role as senior minister at Redeemer to the staff of Redeemer City to City, an organization that helps national church leaders around the world reach and minister in global cities. He is the author of *The Prodigal Prophet, God's Wisdom for Navigating Life*, as well as *The Meaning of Marriage, The Prodigal God*, and *The Reason for God*, among others.

MW00774915

On Death

TIMOTHY KELLER

PENGUIN BOOKS

PENGUIN BOOKS
An imprint of Penguin Random House LLC
penguinrandomhouse.com

All Bible references are from the New International Version
(NIV), unless otherwise noted.

ISBN 9780143135371 (paperback)
ISBN 9780525507031 (ebook)

Printed in the United States of America
2nd Printing

Set in Adobe Garamond Pro with Neutraface
Designed by Sabrina Bowers

Contents

Introduction to the
How to Find God Series · *xi*

Foreword · *xv*

The Fear of Death:
Conscience Makes Cowards of Us All · *1*

The Rupture of Death:
Do Not Grieve Like Those Without Hope · *35*

Appendix · *75*

Acknowledgments · *97*

Notes · *99*

Further Reading · *105*

Introduction to the How to Find God Series

L ife is a journey, and finding and knowing God is fundamental to that journey. When a new child is born, when we approach marriage, and when we find ourselves facing death—either in old age or much earlier—it tends to concentrate the mind. We shake ourselves temporarily free from absorption in the whirl of daily life and ask the big questions of the ages:

Am I living for things that matter?

Will I have what it takes to face this new stage of life?

Do I have a real relationship with God?

The most fundamental transition any human being can make is what the Bible refers to as the new birth (John 3:1–8), or becoming a "new creation" (2 Corinthians 5:17). This can happen at any time in a life, of course, but often the circumstances that lead us to vital faith in Christ occur during these tectonic shifts in life stages. Over forty-five years of ministry, my wife, Kathy, and I have seen that people are particularly open to exploring a relationship with God at times of major life transition.

In this series of short books we want to help readers facing major life changes to think about

what constitutes the truly changed life. Our purpose is to give readers the Christian foundations for life's most important and profound moments. We start with birth and baptism, move into marriage, and conclude with death. Our hope is that these slim books will provide guidance, comfort, wisdom, and, above all, will help point the way to finding and knowing God all throughout your life.

Foreword

As we age, Tim and I find ourselves encountering death, both pastorally and personally, more and more often. Our closest friends and family are now beginning to die. Over the last eighteen months, we have had three deaths in our family; in just the past three months we have talked to both a friend and a family member about how to face their impending deaths. Much of what we say in those conversations is in this book.

The foundation of *On Death* is a sermon preached by my husband at my sister Terry Hall's funeral on January 6, 2018. She died on Christmas Day, at home, surrounded by family after a lengthy struggle with metastatic breast cancer. She knew she was dying and spent time leaving instructions for us on the hymns, prayers, and other elements she wanted for her funeral service. She was adamant that Tim should preach the Gospel at her funeral and not merely talk about her life (as much as we loved and admired her). She knew that "death tends to concentrate the mind wonderfully"[1] and she wanted those present at her funeral to be prepared for their own deaths.

This book is dedicated to her, and to her husband, Bob, and daughters, Ruth Hall Ramsey and Rachael Hall. The sermon that day was, by all accounts, moving and memorable. The request to have it published came from her sisters, Sue and Lynn, and her brother, Steve.

KATHY KELLER
JULY 2018

On Death

The Fear
of Death

Conscience Makes Cowards of Us All

. . . that by his death he might break the power of him who holds the power of death—that is, the devil—and free those who all their lives were held in slavery by their fear of death.

—HEBREWS 2:14-15

D eath is the Great Interruption, tearing loved ones away from us, or us from them.

Death is the Great Schism, ripping apart the material and immaterial parts of our being and sundering a whole person, who was never meant to be disembodied, even for a moment.

Death is the Great Insult, because it reminds us, as Shakespeare said, that we are worm food.[1]

> [We are] literally split in two: [Man] has an awareness of his own splendid uniqueness in that he sticks out of nature with a towering majesty, and yet he goes back into the ground a few feet in order to blindly and dumbly rot and disappear forever.[2]

Death is hideous and frightening and cruel and unusual. It is not the way life is supposed to be, and our grief in the face of death acknowledges that.

Death is our Great Enemy, more than anything. It makes a claim on each and every one of us, pursuing us relentlessly through all our days. Modern people write and talk endlessly about love, especially romantic love, which eludes many. But no one can avoid death. It has been said that all the wars and plagues have never raised the death toll—it has always been one for each and every person. Yet we seem far less prepared for it than our ancestors. Why is that?

The Blessing of Modern Medicine

One reason is, paradoxically, that the great blessing of modern medicine has hidden death from us. Annie Dillard, in her novel *The Living*, devotes an entire page to the astonishing variety of ways death snatched the living from the

3

midst of their homes and families without a moment's notice in the nineteenth century.

> Women took fever and died from having babies, and babies died from puniness or the harshness of the air. Men died from . . . rivers and horses, bulls, steam saws, mill gears, quarried rock, or falling trees or rolling logs. . . . Children lost their lives as . . . hard things smashed them, like trees and the ground when horses threw them, or they fell; they drowned in water; they sickened, and earaches wormed into their brains or fever from measles burned them up or pneumonia eased them out overnight.[3]

Death was something that people used to see

up close. To take just one example, the prominent British minister and theologian John Owen
(1616–1683) outlived every one of his eleven
children, as well as his first wife. Since people
died where they lived, at home, Owen literally
saw nearly every person he loved die before his
eyes. The average family in the United States in
colonial times lost one out of every three children before adulthood. And since the life ex-
pectancy of all people at that time was about
forty years, great numbers lost their parents when
they were still children. Nearly everyone grew
up seeing corpses and watching relatives die,
young and old.[4]

Medicine and science have relieved us of
many causes of early death, and today the vast
majority of people decline and die in hospitals
and hospices, away from the eyes of others. It is
normal now to live to adulthood and not watch

anyone die, or even see a corpse except in the brief glance of an open coffin at a funeral.

Atul Gawande and others have pointed out that this hiddenness of dying in modern society means that we of all cultures live in denial of the inexorability of our impending death. Psalm 90:12 called readers to "number our days" that we may "gain a heart for wisdom." There has always been a danger that humans would live in denial of their own death. Of course we know intellectually and rationally that we are going to die, but deep down we repress it, we act as if we are going to live forever. And, according to the psalmist, that's *not wise.* It is the one absolute inevitability, yet modern people don't plan for it and don't live as if it is going to happen. We avoid doctors out of fear, denying the mortality of our bodies and assuming they will just go on forever. And yet in the face of imminent death we then demand unrealistic and extreme medical procedures.[5] We even find the discussion of death "in bad taste" or worse. Anthropologist Geoffrey Gorer, in his essay "The Pornography of Death," argued that in contemporary culture death has replaced sex as the new unmentionable.[6] .

If people three thousand years ago had a problem with the denial of death, as Psalm 90 attests, then we have an infinitely greater one. Medical progress supports the illusion that death can be put off indefinitely. It is more rare than ever to find people who are, as the ancients were, reconciled to their own mortality. And there are even thinkers now who seriously believe death can be solved like any technological "performance issue."[7] Many in Silicon Valley are obsessed with overcoming mortality and living forever. All this means that modern people are more unrealistic and unprepared for death than any people in history.

This-world Happiness

A second reason that we today struggle so much with death is the secular age's requirement of this-world meaning and fulfillment. Anthropologist Richard Shweder surveys the ways non-Western and older cultures have helped their members face suffering.[8] They all did so by teaching their members about the meaning of life, the main thing for which every person should be living. Many societies believe that the main thing to live for is your people and family—children and grandchildren—in whom you live on after you die. Buddhism and many other ancient Eastern cultures have taught that the meaning of life is to see the illusory nature of this world and therefore to transcend it through an inner calmness and detachment of soul. Other cultures believe in reincarnation, or heaven or nirvana after death, and so one's main purpose is to live and believe in such a way that your soul journeys to heaven.

These all are quite different, and yet, Shweder argues, they had one thing in common. In each case the main thing to live for was something outside this material world and life, some object that suffering and death could not touch. It might be to go to heaven when you die, or to escape the cycle of reincarnation and go into eternal bliss, or to shed the illusion of the world and return to the All Soul of the universe, or to live an honorable life and be received at death into the company of your ancestors. But in each case, not only are tragedy and death unable to destroy your meaning in life, they can actually hasten the journey toward it, whether it is through spiritual growth, or the achievement of honor and virtue, or going into an eternity of joy.

Modern culture, however, is basically secular. Many today say that, because there is no God, soul, or spirit, no transcendent or supernatural dimension to reality, this material world is all there is. In that case, whatever gives your life meaning and purpose will have to be something within the confines of this earthly time frame. You must, as it were, rest your heart in something within the limited horizons of time and space. Whatever you decide will give meaning to your life will have to be some form of this-world happiness, comfort, or achievement. Or, at best, it might be a love relationship.

But death, of course, destroys all of these things. So while other cultures and worldviews see suffering and death as crucial chapters (and not the last) in your coherent life story, the secular view is completely different. Suffering is an interruption and death is the utter end. Shweder writes that for modern people, therefore:

> Suffering is . . . separated from the narrative structure of human life . . . a kind of "noise," an accidental interference into the life drama of the sufferer . . . Suffering [has] no intelligible relation to any plot, except as a chaotic interruption.[9]

Modern culture, then, is the worst in history at preparing its members for the only inevitability—death. When this limited meaning horizon comes together with the advance of medicine, it leaves many people paralyzed with anxiety and fear when confronted with a dying person.

Mark Ashton was vicar of St. Andrew the Great in Cambridge, England. At the age of sixty-two, in late 2008, he was diagnosed with inoperable gallbladder cancer. Because of his faith and joy in Christ, he showed a great deal of confidence in the face of dying and even a sense of anticipation, despite his keen recognition of the sadness of his family. During the next fifteen months, he talked with virtually everyone he met about his coming death with ease, eloquence, and poise. But this unnerved many people, who found not only his attitude but even his presence difficult to take.

He wrote: "Our age is so devoid of hope in the face of death that the topic has become unmentionable." He made a trip to a hairdresser in Eastbourne, where he engaged in conversation as usual with the woman who was cutting his hair. When she "asked me how I was and I replied that I had been told I had got just a few more months to live," the ordinary friendliness and chattiness of the place ceased. No matter how much he tried to talk to her, "I could not get another word out of her for the rest of the haircut."[10] Rather than accept and prepare for the inevitable, we only avert and deny it.

The Sense of Insignificance

A third reason modern secular culture has so much trouble with death is that, in redefining death as nonexistence, it has created a profound sense of insignificance. Ernest Becker, in the Pulitzer Prize–winning *The Denial of Death*, argues human beings cannot accept that all we are—our conscious self, our loves, our profound aspirations for beauty, goodness, truth—is going to cease to exist forever, in a literal blink of an eye. If death is truly the end—if we all die and eventually even the whole human civilization "dies" in the death of the sun—then nothing we do will make any final difference. If we come from nothing and go to nothing, how can we avoid, even now, a sense of nothingness? So he writes:

> The idea of death, the fear of it, haunts the human animal like nothing else; it is the mainspring of human activity— activity designed largely to avoid the

fatality of death, to overcome it by denying . . . that it is the final destiny.[11]

That fear of insignificance in the face of nonexistence *must* be dealt with in some way. Becker cites anthropologists who tell us ancient peoples were much less afraid of death, that death was "accompanied by rejoicing and festivities." He rightly adds that, while fear of death is a human universal, ancient people addressed it through belief in life and meaning after death. They believed in eternity, so that death was "the ultimate promotion." The problem for us today, however, is that "most modern Westerners have trouble believing this any more, which is what makes the fear of death so prominent a part of our psychological make-up."[12]

The rest of Becker's book is based on this

thesis; namely, that modern, secular culture has a problem with death that no other society has faced. He makes a case that the outsize place of so many things in modern culture—of sex and romance, of money and career, of politics and social causes—illustrates the ways that contemporary people seek to get a feeling of significance in the face of death without having recourse to God and religion.

Late-twentieth-century secular thinkers were, like Becker, quite aware that, as religion and faith in God receded, death would pose a problem. The existentialists, such as Albert Camus in "The Myth of Sisyphus," argued that the finality of death made life absurd and to try to deny this fact by losing yourself in pleasure and achievement was wrong.[13] An illustration may help here. Imagine someone has broken into your house, tied you up, and announced that he is going to kill you. For the sake of the illustration imagine also that you have absolutely no hope for rescue. What if he said, "I'm not heartless—tell me something you do that gives you a lot of happiness." You answer that you enjoy playing chess. "Well, let's play a game of chess before I kill you. Won't that make your final moments pleasant?" The only truthful answer would be that your impending death would drain all the satisfaction out of a game. Death takes away the significance and joy of things.

Becker goes further and says that this fear of death is something that is unique to us humans.

> It is a terrifying dilemma to be in and to
> have to live with. The lower animals are,
> of course, spared this painful contradic-
> tion, as they lack a symbolic identity and

the self-consciousness that goes with it. . . . The knowledge of death is reflective and conceptual, and animals are spared it. They [experience death as] a few minutes of fear, a few seconds of anguish, and it is over. But to live a whole lifetime with the fate of death haunting one's dreams and even the most sun-filled days—that's something else.[14]

More recent secular thinkers have not struck such dire notes. Drawing on the ancient philosophers Epicurus and Lucretius, many today argue that death is "nothing to be frightened of," and there is a constant stream of articles posted with that message, such as Jessica Brown's essay in *The Guardian* "We Fear Death, but What If Dying Isn't as Bad as We Think?"[15] After all, the reasoning goes, when you die you simply don't know anything or feel anything. There is no pain or anguish. Why be afraid of it? But efforts to say that modern people should find death no big deal have not worked for most. Philosopher Luc Ferry says it is "brutal" and dishonest to tell people facing death, and therefore the loss of all love relationships, that they should not fear it.[16] Dylan Thomas strikes a far more resonant chord with us when he says we should "Rage, rage against the dying of the light."[17]

Becker is right. The human race as a whole can't *not* fear and hate death. It is a unique and profound problem. Religion gave people tools to help in facing our most formidable foe, and modern secularism has not come up with anything to compensate for its loss.

A Fear of Judgment

A fourth reason why we struggle today with death is the loss of categories for sin, guilt, and forgiveness in modern culture. Friedrich Nietzsche argued that the idea and feeling of "indebtedness" or guilt emerged in human beings along with a belief in a transcendent God or gods to whom we must give obedience. But now, he said happily, as religion recedes and increasing numbers do not believe in a God of judgment, there would be a decline in our sense of guilt. Atheism could even mean "a second innocence."[18]

Wilfred M. McClay, in "The Strange Persistence of Guilt," argues that Nietzsche's prediction has not come true.[19] Freud, McClay says, was a better prophet when he said that guilt is an irreplaceable feature of any civilization. It is the price we must pay if we are going to restrain the kind of selfish behavior that undermines societies. That means that even if we try to end our sense of sinfulness and guilt, it will persist and take other forms. "Guilt is crafty, a trickster and chameleon, capable of disguising itself, hiding out, changing its size and appearance . . . all the while managing to persist and deepen."[20] Freud called guilt *unbehagen*. The word means "malaise," a strong sense of uneasiness about oneself and life itself, which leads to a drumbeat of questions: "Why isn't life better? Why don't I fit in? Why do I feel the need to work so hard to prove myself? Will anybody really love me?"

Our secular culture believes Nietzsche rather than Freud at this point and has done all it can to liberate individuals in order to indulge in complete freedom of self-expression. That means removing the words "sin" and "guilt" from public discourse so everyone can be free to create and perform the self they choose. But this has left us in a strange position. As one scholar put it, we see evil and sin around us, things "that our culture no longer gives us the vocabulary to express," and so "a gulf has opened up in our culture between the visibility of evil and the intellectual resources available for coping with it."[21]

Many have pointed out that today our society is as moralistic and judgmental as it ever has been. We live in a "call-out culture" in which people are categorized reductionistically to good or evil and then are publicly shamed until they lose jobs and communities.[22] People are charged for what used to be called sins and are punished and banished in ways that look remarkably like religious ceremonial purification rites.

As McClay points out, human beings cannot

abandon their moral reflexes—a belief in moral absolutes, in sin and judgment, and in the imposition of guilt and shame. However, today we have abandoned the old underlying beliefs in God, heaven, and hell, and therefore have lost the older resources for repentance, showing grace, and granting forgiveness.[23]

All this triggers a crisis for modern people in the face of death. As a pastor I've spent many hours in the presence of dying people. As death approaches, people look back on their life and feel tremendous regret. The *unbehagen*, or deep dissatisfaction with oneself, comes to the fore. There may be guilt for things not said or done for loved ones, for apologies not made or received, for kindnesses refused or unkindnesses done and now beyond forgiveness, for wasted opportunities or even a wasted life.

But beyond regret for the past, there is also

fear of the future. T. S. Eliot writes: "Not what we call death, but what beyond death is not death / We fear, we fear."[24] Behind and beneath all the other emotions is the fear of judgment. In 1 Corinthians 15, Saint Paul's lengthy discussion of death, he asserts that the "sting of death" is sin (verse 56). Just as he had taught in Romans 1:20–22, we all know in our hearts, however deeply hidden, that God is our Creator and the one who deserves our worship and obedience. But we have "suppressed" (verse 18) that knowledge in order to claim sovereignty over our own lives.

Death, however, makes our self-dissatisfaction much more conscious. Our conscience cannot be silenced as it was before. Shakespeare's Hamlet thinks about suicide, but he decides not to do it. He dreads something after death, "the undiscovered country from whose bourn no traveler returns," which leads us to fear judgment. So we "bear those ills we have, [rather] than fly to others that we know not of" because "conscience does make cowards of us all."[25]

Despite all the efforts, there is a persistence of guilt, and never more than when we face death. Modern culture gives us little to deal with this, but the Christian faith has some astonishing resources for us.

Our Champion

Rather than living in fear of death, we should see it as spiritual smelling salts that will awaken us out of our false belief that we will live forever. When you are at a funeral, especially one for a friend or a loved one, listen to God speaking to you, telling you that everything in life is temporary except for His love. This is reality.

Everything in this life is going to be taken away from us, except one thing: God's love, which can go into death with us and take us through it and into His arms. It's the one thing you can't lose. Without God's love to embrace us, we will always feel radically insecure, and we ought to be.

One of my theology professors, Addison Leitch, told the class about speaking at a missionary conference. Two young women hearing his preaching decided they wanted to give their lives to missionary service. Both sets of their parents were extremely upset with Dr. Leitch, who they felt had filled their children with religious fanaticism. They said to him, "You know that there is no security in being a missionary. The

pay is low, the living situation may be dangerous. We've tried talking to our daughters. They
need to get a job and a career, maybe get a master's degree or something like that so that they
have some security before they go off and do
this missionary thing."

And this is what Dr. Leitch told them: "You
want them to have some security? We're all on a
little ball of rock called Earth, and we're spin-
ning through space at millions of miles an hour.
Someday a trapdoor is going to open up under
every single one of us, and we will fall through
it. And either there will be millions and millions of miles of nothing—or else there will be
the everlasting arms of God. And you want
them to get a master's degree to give them a little security?"[26]

It's in death that God says, "If I'm not your
security, then you've got no security, because

I'm the only thing that can't be taken away from you. I will hold you in my everlasting arms. Every other set of arms will fail you, but I will never fail you."

Smelling salts are very disagreeable, but they are also effective. But as you're waking from your illusions, be at peace, because here's what Jesus Christ offers to us if by faith we have him as our Savior.

In the book of Hebrews we read:

> In bringing many sons and daughters to glory, it was fitting that God, for whom and through whom everything exists, should make the pioneer of their salvation perfect through what he suffered. . . . He too shared in their humanity so that by his death he might

break the power of him who holds the
power of death—that is, the devil—and
free those who all their lives were held
in slavery by their fear of death. (Hebrews 2:10, 14–15)

In order to save us, Jesus became the "pio-
neer" of our salvation through suffering and
death. The Greek word here is *archēgos*. Bible
scholar William Lane says it really ought to be
translated "our champion."[27]

A champion was somebody who engaged in
representative combat. When David fought Go-
liath, they both fought as champions for their
respective armies. They fought as substitutes. If
your champion won, the whole army won the
battle, even though none of them lifted a finger.
That is what Jesus did. He took on our greatest

enemies—sin and death. Unlike David, he didn't just risk his life, he gave his life, but in doing so he defeated them. He took the penalty we deserve for our sins—the punishment of death—in our place, as our substitute. But because he himself was a man of perfect, sinless love for God and neighbor, death could not hold him (Acts 2:24). He rose from the dead.

That's why in Hebrews 2:14, the writer says he destroyed the power of death because he died for us, taking away our penalty and guaranteeing the future resurrection of all who unite with him by faith. Jesus Christ, our great captain and champion, has killed death.

All religions talk about death and the afterlife, but in general they proclaim that you must lead a good life in order to be ready for eternity. Yet as death approaches we all know we have not even come close to doing our best; we have not lived as we ought. So we stay, with warrant, enslaved by the fear of death until the end.

Christianity is different. It doesn't leave you to face death on your own, by holding up your life record and hoping it will suffice. Instead it gives you a champion who has defeated death, who pardons you and covers you with his love. You face death "in him" and with *his* perfect record (Philippians 3:9). To the degree we believe, know, and embrace that, we are released from the power of death.

So when Hamlet spoke of death as "the undiscovered country from whose bourn no traveler returns" he was wrong. Someone *has* come back from death. Jesus Christ has destroyed the power of death and "a cleft has opened in the pitiless walls of the world" for us.[28] When by faith we grasp this, we need fear darkness no more.

Saint Paul wrote the famous lines:

> Where, O death, is your victory?
> Where, O death, is your sting?
> (1 Corinthians 15:55)

Paul is not facing death stoically. He's *taunt-ing* it. How can anyone in his right mind look at humanity's most powerful enemy *and taunt it*? Paul immediately gives the answer: "The sting of death is sin, and the power of sin is the law. But thanks be to God! He gives us the victory through our Lord Jesus Christ" (1 Corinthians 15:56–57). Paul says that the "sting of death" (as Hamlet says) is our conscience, our sense of sin and judgment before the moral law. But Christ has taken it away—or more accurately, taken it upon himself for all who believe.

Donald Grey Barnhouse was the minister of

Tenth Presbyterian Church in Philadelphia when his wife, only in her late thirties, died of cancer, leaving him with four children under the age of twelve. When driving with his children to the funeral, a large truck pulled past them in the left lane, casting its shadow over them. Barnhouse asked all in the car, "Would you rather be run over by the truck or the shadow of the truck?" His eleven-year-old answered, "Shadow, of course." Their father concluded, "Well, that's what has happened to your mother. . . . Only the shadow of death has passed over her, because death itself ran over Jesus."[29]

The sting of death is sin, and the poison went into Jesus.

So any Christian man or woman has the power to triumph over death like this. Once I was speaking to a friend about his chronically ill wife, who over and over again had defied medical predictions and had "beaten death." Now she was very ill again, with a real possibility that this time she would not pull through. Talking with her husband, we agreed that no matter what happened a believer *always* beats death whether they die or not. Jesus Christ has defeated death, and now all it can do is make us more happy and loved than we've ever been. If Jesus died for you and he has risen to be your living Savior, then what can death do to you?

The Rupture
of Death

Do Not Grieve Like
Those Without Hope

Brothers and sisters, we do not want you to . . .
grieve like the rest of mankind, who have no hope.
For we believe that Jesus died and rose again, and
so we believe that God will bring with Jesus those
who have fallen asleep in him.

—1 THESSALONIANS 4:13-14

I n our first chapter we talked about how to
face your own death without fear. But how
do we face the death of loved ones? I can say
without fear of contradiction there will be a lot

of death in your future. If you are fortunate enough to live a long life, you will be encountering death more and more as you go on—the death of not just associates but friends, and not just friends but dearly loved ones. In 1 Thessalonians 4 we are told that Christianity gives us remarkable resources—not only for your own death, but for the loss of people we love.

In the epigraph above, Saint Paul tells his friends: "I don't want you to grieve like the rest of humanity, who have no hope." That's a double negative. He is actually saying, "I want you to *grieve hopefully*." Saint Paul is calling for an extreme balance before our Great Enemy. When we think of someone who is "balanced" that usually means a person who avoids extremes, but Paul is calling us to a balanced combination *of* two extremes. Notice he does not say, "Don't grieve." He wants Christians to grieve when loved ones die, but in a particular way. He says neither, "Instead of grieving I want you to have hope," nor "There's really no hope, so just cry and grieve." Rather, he says Christians can and must both grieve profoundly and fully and yet do so with hope. How does that work?

We Are to Grieve

On the one hand we are to grieve rather than take the stoic approach. But although grieving is right, grief can become bitterness; it can embitter you, darken your life, and stifle joy unless you season it with hope. The most remarkable example of this is Jesus at the tomb of Lazarus, his friend, in John 11. Jesus did not come up to Mary and Martha, the bereaved sisters, and say, "There, there. Keep a stiff upper lip. Chin up.

Be strong." He didn't do any of that. When Mary speaks to him, we are told, in the shortest verse in the Bible, "Jesus wept" (John 11:35). He doesn't speak—all he does is weep. And then, when he goes to Lazarus's tomb (though all the English translations mute this), we are told that Jesus was "snorting with rage" (John 11:38).[1]

Here is Jesus, the Son of God, who knew quite well that he was going to do a great miracle and raise his friend from the dead. We would think, would we not, that he would be walking to the tomb quietly smiling and thinking to himself, "Wait till you see what I'm going to do! Everything is going to be fine!" Instead he is weeping, grieving, angry.

How could the Creator of the world be angry at something in his world? Only if death is an intruder. Death was not in God's original design for the world and human life. Look at the first three chapters of Genesis. We were not meant to die; we were meant to last. We were meant to get more and more beautiful as time goes on, not more and more enfeebled. We were meant to get stronger, not to weaken and die. Paul explains elsewhere, in Romans 8:18–23, that when we turned from God to be our own Lords and Saviors, everything broke. Our bodies, the natural order, our hearts, our relationships—nothing works the way it was originally designed. It is all marred, distorted, broken, and death is part of that (Genesis 3:7–19). So Jesus weeps and is angry at the monstrosity of death. It is a deep distortion of the creation he loves.

Therefore, the stoic, "keep a stiff upper lip" reaction to death and grief is wrong. There are many versions of this. One goes like this: "Now, now. He is with the Lord. The Lord works all things together for good. There's no need to weep too much. Of course you will miss him, but he's in heaven now. And everything happens for a reason." Technically there may be nothing wrong with any of these statements. They may be true. But Jesus knew all of them as well. He knew Lazarus was going to be raised. He knew that this was part of the Father's plan for his ministry. And he was still grieving with sorrow and anger. Why? Because that is the right response to the evil and unnaturalness of death.

Most secular advice for the bereaved is some version of stoicism. An ancient example is in the *Iliad*, where Achilles tells the father of the fallen Hector, "Bear up . . . Nothing will come of sorrowing for your son."[2] Modern skeptics will say, "Look, death is the end, and that's it. Grieving about it makes no difference. It doesn't help a thing. It is what it is."

A somewhat more sophisticated modern version of the secular view tells us to look at death as a perfectly natural part of the life cycle. It says: "Death is natural. Death is just a part of life. Death is nothing to be afraid of. Our bodies enrich the earth like the grass, trees, and other animals when we die. Eventually we become stardust. We're still part of the universe. It's okay." But does such a view of death fit our deepest intuitions?

Peter Kreeft is a Christian philosopher who tells a story about a couple who were friends of his and who were not religious people. They had a seven-year-old son whose three-year-old cousin had died.

So they sat down and tried to comfort him. They said, "You realize death is perfectly natural." They were trying to help him by explaining, "Death is fine, it is perfectly natural. When you die, your body goes to the earth and enriches the earth and other things grow. Remember, you watched *The Lion King*."

But instead of being comforted, the little boy ran out of the room screaming, "I don't want him to be fertilizer!"[3]

The little boy was closer to Jesus's point of view than his parents were. He was grieving. Death is not right. It's not the way it ought to be. It's not the way God made the world.

To say, "Oh, death is just natural," is to harden and perhaps kill a part of your heart's hope that makes you human. We know deep down that we are not like trees or grass. We were created to *last*. We don't want to be ephemeral, to be inconsequential. We don't want to just be a wave upon the sand. The deepest desires of our hearts are for love that lasts.

Death is not the way it ought to be. It is abnormal, it is not a friend, it isn't right. This isn't truly part of the circle of life. Death is the end of it. So grieve. Cry. The Bible tells us not only to weep, but to weep with those who are weeping (Romans 12:15 NASB). We have a lot of crying to do.

We Are to Grieve with Hope

However, though we are definitely right to grieve, Saint Paul says we must grieve with hope. As we have seen, to suppress grief and outrage at death is not only bad for us psychologically, it's actually bad for our humanity. Yet anger can dehumanize us, too, making us bitter and hard. Which means that we cannot *only* "rage against the dying of the light." We also need a hope that influences how we grieve.

But what is there to hope for? Look at Jesus Christ at the tomb of his friend Lazarus. He's grieving, he's weeping, and he's angry, even though he knows that in a few minutes he will raise his friend from the dead.

But he knows something that no one else could even imagine. At the end of chapter 11 of John, after he raised his friend Lazarus from the dead, all of his opponents said, "Well, that's the last straw. We've got to kill him now. We've got to kill Jesus."

Jesus knew that to raise Lazarus from the dead would push his enemies toward extreme measures. So he knew that the only way he could get Lazarus out of the tomb was if he put himself into it. Indeed, if he is to guarantee resurrection for all who believe in him, he must put himself into the grave. On the Cross that's what he did.

Because of Jesus's death, we are released from sin and death, and share in his resurrection, as it says in Romans 6:5–9:

> For if we have been united with him in a death like his, we will certainly also be united with him in a resurrection like his. For we know that our old self was crucified with him so that the body ruled by sin might be done away with, that we should no longer be slaves to sin—because anyone who has died has been set free from sin. Now if we died with Christ, we believe that we will also live with him. For we know that since Christ was raised from the dead, he cannot die again; death no longer has mastery over him.

Jesus conquered death, and we will share in his resurrection. That's our hope.

If you don't have that hope, I'm not sure what you do when you are in the presence of death. You can let it fester and cause despair. Or we can add hope to our grief.

We tend to see grief and hope as mutually exclusive, but Paul does not. An illustration may help to see how these can go together. For many years, people preserved meat by salting it. (If you have ever had country ham you know this is still a method of preservation.) Salt cured the meat so it didn't decay.

Similarly, unless you salt your grief with hope, your grief will go bad.

When we grieve and rage in the face of death, we are responding appropriately to a great evil. But Christians have a hope that can be "rubbed into" our sorrow and anger the way salt is rubbed into meat. Neither stifling grief nor giving way to despair is right. Neither repressed anger nor unchecked rage is good for your soul. But pressing hope into your grief makes you wise, compassionate, humble, and tenderhearted.

Grieve fully yet with profound hope! Do you see why I said that this is not some midpoint moderation but a combination of extremes? This will give you more strength than stoicism and more freedom to lament than hopelessness.

I had my first personal experience of this many years ago. There was a nodule on my thyroid gland that was being biopsied. I was in the clinic when the pathologist said to me, "You have a carcinoma." The shocked look on my face was the reason she then said, "I'm sure it's treatable!" My thyroid cancer turned out to indeed be treatable. Nevertheless, over the next few months I learned that it is one thing to tell people "Christians have hope in the face of death," and it's another thing to grasp that hope personally and practically when you know you have a cancer that can kill you.

I discovered that one of the keys to getting access to this Christian hope was to ponder what Saint Paul said about how he didn't want his friends to grieve "like the rest of mankind, who have no hope." Some commentators have pointed out that there are many religions and almost all of them believe in some kind of life after death. So how can Paul say that the rest of the human race has no hope in the face of death?

As others have pointed out, Paul is speaking relatively. When Jesus says in Luke 14:26 that his followers should "hate father and mother" he means their devotion to him should be so great that it makes all other loyalties pale and look like hate in comparison. Likewise Paul is not saying that no one has any expectation of life after death, but that the Christian future hope is uniquely powerful. He is calling us to delight in the greatness of our hope in order to prepare ourselves for death.

The Power of Christian Hope

What then are some of the features of this unique hope we have in the face of death?

Personal Hope

It's a personal hope. The future of those who die in Christ is a world of infinite love. There are religions that say, "Yes, there is life after death, but you lose your personal consciousness. You lose your sense of individuality, which was an illusion anyway. It's like you're a drop going back into the ocean. You don't remain a drop. You just become part of the All Soul. There is not a *you* or a *me* after death, but you continue as part of the universe."

But Paul goes on to say:

> For the Lord himself will come down from heaven, with a loud command, with the voice of the archangel and with the trumpet call of God, and the dead in Christ will rise first. After that, we who are still alive and are left will be caught up together with them in the clouds to meet the Lord in the air. And so we will be with the Lord forever.

Therefore encourage each other with these words. (Thessalonians 4:16–18)

Notice all the references that we will be *with* one another. You will be with people you've lost. And do you see the word "together"? We will be with the Lord together forever. These are words that mean personal relationships—perfect relationships of love that go on forever.

Jonathan Edward's famous sermon "Heaven Is a World of Love" begins by arguing that the greatest happiness we can know is to be loved by another person, and yet, he adds, on earth the greatest love relationships are like a pipe so clogged that only a little water (or love) actually gets through. In heaven, however, all these "clogs" are removed and the love we will experience will be infinitely, inexpressibly greater than anything we have known here.[4] On earth we hide behind facades for fear of being rejected, but that means we never experience the transforming power of being fully known yet truly loved at the same time. In addition, we love selfishly and enviously, which disrupts, weakens, and even ends love relationships. Finally, our love relationships are darkened by the fear of losing the other person, which can make us so controlling that we often drive people away, or in other cases become fearful of making any commitments at all.

Edwards concludes by declaring that all of these things that reduce love in this world to a trickle at the bottom of a riverbed are removed when we get to heaven, where love is an endless deluge and fountain of delight and bliss flowing in and out of us infinitely and eternally.

The Christian hope is for a personal future of love relationships.

Material Hope

Our hope is also material. Notice that Paul does not say merely that we will go to heaven. He says that the "dead in Christ will rise." Yes, we believe our souls go to heaven when we die, but that isn't the climactic end of our salvation. At the end of all things, we will get new bodies. We will be raised like Jesus was raised. Remember that when the risen Jesus met his disciples he insisted that he had "flesh and bones," that he was not a spirit. He ate in front of them to prove the point (Luke 24:37–43). He taught them that, unlike all other major religions, Christianity promises not a spirit-only future, but a renewed heavens and earth, a perfected material world from which all suffering and tears, disease, evil, injustice, and death have been eliminated.

Our future is not an immaterial one. We are not going to float in the kingdom of God like ghosts. We're going to walk, eat, hug, and be hugged. We're going to love. We're going to sing, because we're going to have vocal cords. And we will do all this in degrees of joy, excellence, satisfaction, beauty, and power we cannot now imagine. We're going to eat and drink with the Son of Man.

And this is the final defeat of death. This is not merely a consolation in heaven for the material life we lost. This is a restoration of that life. It's getting the love, the body, the mind, the being we've always longed for.

You see, there's a real you, a true self down inside you, but then there are all the flaws and weaknesses that bury and mar and hide it. But the Christian hope is that the love and holiness of God will burn it all away. On that day, we're going to see each other, and say, "I always knew you could be like this. I saw glimpses of it. I saw flashes of it. Now look at you."

Paul, knowing something about the other cultures and religions of the world, says our future is not an impersonal, immaterial world of abstract spirituality, but a personal future of love relationships and the restoration of all things.

If the knowledge of this future was always present in our minds, would we become as downcast as we do? Why ever think of payback for people who have wronged you when you know you're going to get not just all you've ever wanted, but more than you dare ask or think? Why envy anyone? This hope is transforming.

Beatific Hope

Along with personal hope and material hope, there is beatific hope. Paul does not say we will simply be together with others. Nor does he talk so much about how lovely the world will be when it's healed. That's not the main thing in his mind. Here's the final note, the biggest emphasis—that we will be "with *the Lord* forever" (1 Thessalonians 4:17). It means we will be in perfect communion with him, we will see the Lord face-to-face. This is what has been historically called the "beatific vision."

Paul talks about it in 1 Corinthians 13:12 when he says, "For now we see only a reflection as in a mirror; then we shall see face to face. Now I know in part; then I shall know fully, even as I am fully known." John speaks of it in 1 John 3:2 when he says, "We know that when

Christ appears, we shall be like him, for we shall see him as he is." When we look into the face of Christ it will completely transform us because, as Paul says, we will finally be fully known yet fully loved.

When Moses asked in fear and trembling to see God's glory (Exodus 33:18), God replied that for any human being to see God's glory directly would be fatal (Exodus 33:19–20). Sinful human beings cannot come into the presence of a holy God and live. But Moses certainly knew the danger. Why did he seek this direct sight of God's glory anyway? Because he intuitively knew that we were originally created to know and love God supremely, to commune with his love and see his beauty. Moses knew at some level that our human restlessness and drive— for approval, comfort, aesthetic experience, love, power, accomplishment—are all ways of filling

what Saint Augustine famously called the
"God-shaped hole" in us. In every set of arms
we are seeking God's arms, in every loving face
we are seeking God's face, in every accomplishment we are looking for God's approval.

Moses was after the beatific vision, the direct, face-to-face relationship with God we were
made for. God's answer to Moses is essentially
the theme of the rest of the Bible and of the
gospel itself. God told him that he would have
to be covered or hidden in the cleft of a rock so
he would only be able to see God's "back" (Exodus 33:19–23). In the Old Testament we see
God's glory residing in the tabernacle's Holy of
Holies, present among his people but largely in-
accessible.

But when Jesus comes, John announces that
in Christ "we beheld his glory" (John 1:14), and
Paul adds that because of Jesus's death and work

on our behalf, those of us who believe in him
get a foretaste, by faith, of that future transforming vision. He writes:

> For God, who said, "Let light shine out
> of darkness," made his light shine in
> our hearts to give us the light of the
> knowledge of God's glory displayed in
> the face of Christ. (2 Corinthians 4:6)

This is not the direct, face-to-face encounter
that Moses asked for and that Paul and John
say is still in the future. Rather it is a "faith-
sight" that we can have now. We cannot see
God's glory yet with our physical eyes, but
through faith, the Word and the Spirit can give
us a powerful sense of his presence and reality
in our lives and hearts. Sometimes we read the
promises and truths of Scripture and Jesus

becomes overpoweringly real and consoling to us. Paul talks of it like this:

> And we all, who with unveiled faces contemplate the Lord's glory, are being transformed into his image with ever-increasing glory, which comes from the Lord, who is the Spirit. (2 Corinthians 3:18)

What Paul is talking about is far more rare than it should be, but it is not an experience reserved for a few saints. In Romans he writes: "Hope does not put us to shame, because God's love has been poured out into our hearts through the Holy Spirit, who has been given to us" (Romans 5:5). Our future hope, he argues, is strengthened the more we do not merely know intellectually about the love of God but have it poured into our heart—experienced—through the Holy Spirit. Many have felt what Paul is talking about. You may be reading the Bible or praying or singing his praise and you get a sense of his greatness and love. It is only partial, only by faith, but it comforts and changes you. It's the light of his face shining in our hearts. William Cowper wrote:

> Sometimes a light surprises
> The Christian while he sings;
> It is the Lord Who rises
> With healing in His wings.[5]

C. S. Lewis says if these lower reaches of the stream of God's glory are so intoxicating, what will it be like to drink from the fountainhead?[6]

This is what we are built for. Psalm 16 ends with a sentence that says, literally, "In your face is fullness of joy. At your right hand are pleasures forevermore" (Psalm 16:11). Psalm 17:15 says that after death, "When I awake I will be satisfied with seeing your likeness." John Flavel, a British minister and theologian from the seventeenth century, wrote about Psalm 17:15 and the vision of God that is in our future. He said:

> It will be a satisfying sight (Psalm 17:15). . . . The understanding can know no more, the will can will no more, the affections of joy, delight, and love are at full rest and quiet in their proper center. . . . All that delights you in earthly things can never satisfy you—for all your desires are eminently for God himself. . . . The comforts you had here are but only drops inflaming, not satisfying, the appetites of your soul: but *the Lamb . . . shall lead them to*

fountains of living waters. (Revelation 7:17)[7]

Kathy sometimes says to me, "One of the great things about future glory is you don't have to buy souvenirs." Do you know what she means? You don't live with regrets. You don't say, "I never got any photos when I went to that country," or "I never had this or that experience." Anything wonderful or great in this world is only an echo or foretaste of what is present in the Vision of God and in the New Heaven and New Earth, the world of love.

When at last you see the God of the universe looking at you with love, all of the potentialities of your soul will be released and you will experience the glorious freedom of the children of God.

Assured Hope

There is one more aspect of hope available to Christians that is unique. While other religions may have a belief in an afterlife, there is no firm assurance offered as to who will enjoy it. Theocritus wrote: "Hopes are for the living; the dead are without hope."[8] Other religions can offer no person an assurance that they are virtuous enough to merit a good existence in the next life.[9]

However, Paul writes:

> We believe that Jesus died and rose again, and so we believe that God will bring with Jesus those who have fallen asleep in him. (1 Thessalonians 4:14)

What is Paul talking about? The wages of sin

is death (Romans 6:23)—that is what we deserve. When a prisoner has fully paid his debt he is released; the law no longer has any claim on him. So when Jesus fully paid the debt of sin with his death, he was resurrected. The law and death had no more claim on him. Nor does it have any claim on us if we believe in him. "There is now no condemnation for those who are in Christ Jesus" (Romans 8:1). When we put our faith in him we are as free from condemnation as if we had paid the penalty ourselves—as if we had died. "Now if we died with Christ, we believe that we shall also live with him" (Romans 6:8). That's what Paul is saying here in 1 Thessalonians 4. We not only know about the future world of love, the vision of God, and a renewed universe. We are assured that these astounding things are ours. We do not anxiously wonder if we have been good enough to be with

God when we die. We live with deep assurance of all of these things. This, too, is part of our unequaled Christian hope.

What more could we ask for?

In Mark, chapter 5, Jesus is brought into a room with a little dead girl. Everybody else is wailing in grief, but he's calm. He sits down and he takes her by the hand. The eyewitness account preserves the actual Aramaic words that Jesus Christ spoke to her. He said, *Talitha koum*, which is best translated, "Honey, get up." And she got up.

Jesus sits down, takes her by the hand, and speaks to her the way any father or mother would speak to a child on a sunny morning. Jesus says, "Honey, it's time to get up."

What is Jesus Christ facing at that moment? He is facing the most formidable, inexorable, implacable force that the human race has to face: death.

And with a little tug of his hand, he lifts her right up through it! It's his way of saying, "If I have you by the hand, if you know me through faith in grace, nothing can hurt you. Even death itself, when it comes to you, will just be like waking from a nice night's sleep. If I have you by the hand, even death, when it comes upon you, will only make you something greater. Nothing can hurt you. Be at peace."

C. S. Lewis says, "He will make the feeblest and filthiest of us into . . . a dazzling, radiant, immortal creature, pulsating all through with such energy and joy and wisdom and love as we cannot now imagine, a bright stainless mirror which reflects back to God perfectly (though, of course, on a smaller scale) His own boundless power and delight and goodness. . . . That is what we are in for. Nothing less."[10]

We Are to Laugh and Sing for Joy

In our culture one of the few places where it is acceptable to talk about death is at a funeral. People attend funerals for different reasons. One, of course, is to honor the person who has died and to pay tribute to a unique life. But also your mind is forced to dwell on ultimate things. Just as people think about their own weddings (either in remembrance or in anticipation) when attending a wedding, a funeral confronts you with the fact that one day it will be your funeral people are attending. This tends to turn minds toward questions of the reality of God and the afterlife, even if those thoughts usually don't

The Rupture of Death

arise. But after the funeral is over, unless the deceased was a close family member or friend, the mind goes back to its default setting to keep thoughts about death as far away as possible.

At a funeral service (as opposed to a memorial service) we are literally in the presence of death. There is a dead body in that coffin. While people have many reactions to being in the presence of death, there are two opposite mistakes we can make: One is to despair too much; the other is to shrug it off and not learn what we should from it.

Neither will be of much benefit to you, so we must do as the Bible tells us to do: We should grieve, yet we should have hope; we should wake up from our denial and discover a source of peace that will not leave us; and finally, we should laugh and sing.

The Bible says that when the Son of God

returns, the mountains and the woods will sing for joy. When the Son of God rises with healing in his wings, when Jesus Christ comes back, the Bible says the mountains and the trees will sing for joy, because in his hands we finally become everything God intended us to be.

And if it's true that the mountains and the trees will sing for joy, what will we be able to do?

One of the great expressions of the Christian hope in literature is a poem by George Herbert, a seventeenth-century Christian poet. He wrote a poem called "A Dialogue-Anthem." With elegance and power it imagines a dialogue between Death and a Christian, based on 1 Corinthians 15.

DIALOGUE-ANTHEM
by George Herbert

CHRISTIAN: *Alas, poor Death! Where is thy glory?*
    Where is thy famous force, thy ancient sting?

DEATH: Alas, poor mortal, void of story!
    Go spell and read how I have kill'd thy King.

CHRISTIAN: *Poor death! and who was hurt*
    thereby?
    Thy curse being laid on him makes thee ac-
    curst.

DEATH: Let losers talk, yet thou shalt die:
    These arms shall crush thee.

CHRISTIAN: *Spare not, do thy worst. I shall*
    be one day better than before: Thou so
    much worse, that thou shalt be no more.

Here's the Christian looking at Death and
saying, "Come on, spare not, do thy worst,

come on. Hit me with your best shot. The lower you lay me, the higher you will raise me. The harder you hit me, the more brilliant and glorious I'll be." Elsewhere George Herbert says, "Death used to be an executioner, but the Gospel makes him just a gardener." Death used to be able to crush us, but now all death can do is plant us in God's soil so we become something extraordinary.

Years ago, when the famous Chicago minister Dwight Moody was dying, he said: "Pretty soon you're going to read in the Chicago papers that Dwight Moody is dead. Don't you believe it. I will be more alive than I am right now."

Grieve with hope; wake up and be at peace; laugh in the face of death, and sing for joy at what's coming. If Jesus Christ has you by the hand, you can sing.

A Prayer

Our Father, you are the strength of your people, and we ask now that you would heal the brokenhearted among us and bind up their wounds. We ask that you would grant to them and to all else the vision of that life in which all tears are wiped away and all shadows have fled away.

Raise us up in your Spirit's power now to follow you in hope and trust, and give us your loving power to protect us, your wise power to nurture us, your beauty to enrapture us, your peace to fulfill us, and lift up our hearts in the light and love of your presence. And we ask in the name of the one who is the Resurrection and the Life, Jesus Christ. Amen.

Appendix

If you are facing
your own possible death

The Christian faith gives believers unparalleled promises and hopes in the face of death. We should always be in prayer for healing, because we have an all-powerful, prayer-hearing God. But we should also be ready to meet God face-to-face at any time. This is our opportunity to do both—prayer and preparation.

Do you believe that Jesus came to be your Savior, to live the life you should have lived and also to die in your place in order to atone for your sins and provide salvation as a free gift of grace? Have you turned and repented for all you have done wrong? Do you trust and rest in him alone for your acceptance before God?

If you have this faith, then you will not face God's condemnation (Romans 8:1).

If you're still having trouble experiencing God's comfort and assurance of love in the face of death, ask yourself: Are you clear in your mind about the difference between salvation by faith in Christ's work and record rather than your own? Could it be that in subtle ways your heart still clings in part to the belief that we need to earn our salvation? Then memories of past moral failures will darken your heart. Refuse those thoughts and meditate on Philippians 3:4–9. Paul says here that if anyone should have "confidence in the flesh"—the belief that good works could merit eternal life—it should be him. He was the most religiously and morally zealous person that he knew of. But he realized that all of these things were useless. All that matters is to "be found in him, not having a righteousness [moral record] of my own that comes from the law, but that which is through faith in Christ—the righteousness that comes from God on the basis of faith."

There are many biblical promises for believers to meditate on as they face death. Here are some texts to consider over the course of a week when contemplating or facing your own death. There are seven—one for each day:

Monday. "I eagerly expect and hope that I will in no way be ashamed, but will have sufficient courage so that now as always Christ will be exalted in my body, whether by life or by death. For to me, to live is Christ and to die is gain. If I am to go on living in the body, this will mean fruitful labor for me. Yet what shall I choose? I do not know! I am torn between the two" (Philippians 1:20–23). *While the Bible tells us that death is a tragic monstrosity, yet for Christians with assurance of their relationship with God, it is a win-win. There are unique ways to serve and enjoy God both here and in heaven. Paul is not lying when he says he is "torn between the two."*

Tuesday. "But now, this is what the LORD says— . . . 'Do not fear, for I have redeemed you; I have summoned you by name; you are mine. When you pass through the waters, I will be with you; and when you pass through the rivers, they will not sweep over you. When you walk through the fire, you will not be burned; the flames will not set you ablaze. For I am the

LORD your God, the Holy One of Israel, your Savior'" (Isaiah 43:1–3). *God is saying plainly that, if we are his, he will never let us go. When we suffer here, it will only make us into something more beautiful, the way that pressure creates a diamond. And if we die, it is merely a dark door into ultimate joy. Consider this hymn, based on Isaiah 43.*

> That soul that on Jesus has leaned for repose
> I will not, I will not desert to its foes.
> That soul though all hell should endeavor to shake
> I'll never, no never, no never forsake.[1]

Wednesday. "Therefore we do not lose heart. Though outwardly we are wasting away, yet inwardly we are being renewed day by day. For our light and momentary troubles are achieving for us an eternal glory that far outweighs them all. So we fix our eyes not on what is seen, but on what is unseen, since what is seen is temporary, but what is unseen is eternal" (2 Corinthians 4:16–18). *If we live to old age we can feel our bodies (and our beauty) fading, yet if we are growing in God's grace, our souls, as it were, are becoming stronger and more beautiful. At death this reversal becomes complete. Our bodies disintegrate and we become blindingly glorious. Comfort yourself with these words.*

Thursday. "For we know that if the earthly tent we live in is destroyed, we have a building from God, an eternal house in heaven, not built by human hands. . . . For while we are in this tent, we groan and are burdened, because we do not wish to be unclothed but to be clothed instead with our heavenly dwelling, so that what is mortal may be swallowed up by life. . . . We are confident, I say, and would prefer to be away from the body and at home with the LORD. So we make it our goal to please him, whether we are at home in the body or away from it" (2 Corinthians 5:1, 4, 8–9). *It is reported that an army chaplain, comforting a frightened soldier before a battle, told him: "If you live, Jesus will be with you, but if you die, you will be with him. Either way he has you."*

Friday. "Do not let your hearts be troubled. You believe in God; believe also in me. My Father's house has many rooms; if that were not so, would I have told you that I am going there to prepare a place for you? And if I go and prepare a place for you, I will come back and take you to be with me that you also may be where

I am. . . . Peace I leave with you; my peace I give you. I do not give to you as the world gives. Do not let your hearts be troubled and do not be afraid" (John 14:1–3, 27). *The world can only give us peace that says, "It probably won't get that bad." Jesus's peace is different. It says, "Even the worst that can happen—your death—is ultimately the best thing that can happen. We all long for a "place" that is truly home. Jesus says that it awaits you.*

Saturday. "If we claim to be without sin, we deceive ourselves and the truth is not in us. If we confess our sins, he is faithful and just and will forgive us our sins and purify us from all unrighteousness. . . . I write this to you so that you will not sin. But if anybody does sin, we have an advocate with the Father—Jesus Christ,

the Righteous One" (1 John 1:8–2:1). *If we refuse to admit and try to cover up our sin, God will
uncover it. If we will without excuse repent and
uncover it, then God will have it covered in the
most astonishing way. Believers know that Christ,
as it were, stands before the divine bar of justice
and is our "advocate" or defense attorney. That is,
when God the judge sees us, he sees us "in Christ"
and our sins cannot condemn us. Christians have
nothing to fear from death or judgment.*

Sunday. "For I consider that the sufferings of
this present time are not worth comparing with
the glory that is to be revealed to us. . . . What
then shall we say to these things? If God is for
us, who can be against us? He who did not
spare his own Son but gave him up for us all,
how will he not also with him graciously give us

all things? Who shall bring any charge against God's elect? It is God who justifies. Who is to condemn? Christ Jesus is the one who died—more than that, who was raised—who is at the right hand of God, who indeed is interceding for us. Who shall separate us from the love of Christ? Shall tribulation, or distress, or persecution, or famine, or nakedness, or danger, or sword? . . . No, in all these things we are more than conquerors through him who loved us. For I am sure that neither death nor life, nor angels nor rulers, nor things present nor things to come, nor powers, nor height nor depth, nor anything else in all creation, will be able to separate us from the love of God in Christ Jesus our Lord" (Romans 8:18, 31–35, 37–39 ESV). *The answer to Paul's question is "Nothing! Nothing in Heaven or Earth or anywhere can separate us from the love of God in Christ!" We stand over the coffins of our loved ones, or contemplate our own future death, and are confident that nothing is able to separate us from God.*

If you are facing
the death of a loved one

If the death was sudden, don't feel you have to make major life decisions right away, such as where you will live or whether you will change your job. It probably is not a good time to make these decisions. If the loved one has died after a very long illness—or even after a time in which he or she was unconscious or confused—you often begin doing the work of "letting them go" in your heart before they pass away. But if the death comes as an unexpected shock, an air of unreality can cling to you for a good while. It's a sense that you are in a dream or a movie or that you are somebody else. In such a condition, just take it one day at a time, "doing the next thing," not spending too much time with people or too little. As the reality sinks in and you finally begin to let them go, you'll be in a better position to think about your future. But don't do that too quickly.

Be honest about your thoughts and feelings, whether to others, to God, or even to yourself. Don't feel it is "unspiritual" to question and cry out. Remember Jesus weeping and angry at the death of his friend Lazarus. Remember Job crying out to the Lord. Job complained loudly—but he complained to God. He never stopped praying or meeting with God, even though he was not getting much out of it at the time. Just because we know a loved one is with Christ and eventually we will all be together doesn't mean that somehow we should all just be happy now and should stifle our grief and even our anger. Not at all. Jesus didn't stifle his! Nevertheless, don't express emotion in a completely untempered way that would damage you or people around you.

When we have lost a believing loved one, do meditate on the joy he or she has now. When C. S. Lewis's wife died, he heard someone say, "She's in God's hand," and suddenly he got a picture:

> "She is in God's hand." That gains a new energy when I think of her as a sword. Perhaps the earthly life I shared with her was only part of the tempering. Now perhaps He grasps the hilt; weighs the new weapon; makes lightnings with it in the air. "A right Jerusalem

blade." . . . How wicked it would be, if
we could, to call the dead back![2]

If we actually could physically see our loved
ones now, they would be so radiant and beautiful beyond bearing that we would be tempted
to fall down and worship them. Not that they
would let us.

The biggest challenge after losing a loved one
is to realize that the love, joy, and grace that
seem now to be gone are still available, directly from the original source, the Lord himself. There are depths, fountains of power
available in fellowship with Him that you
haven't even tapped. This is not something that
will happen immediately. Don't expect your
prayer life to feel very good now. It will have
the same air of unreality that everything else

does. But eventually, there is comfort and peace available beyond your wildest imagination. When we have other things—spouse, family, friends, health, home, security—we are not driven to really plumb the depths of what is available in communion and prayer. But there are infinite stores of grace. More than enough to get you through the rest of your life—and as a deeper and wiser and even more joyful person (in some ways) than you were before the tragedy. This kind of wound in some ways never goes away. But, like the nail prints in Jesus's hands, they can become "rich wounds . . . in beauty glorified."[3] Have hope that you won't have to always feel as empty as you do now.

Here are some texts to meditate on over the course of a week when facing the death of a loved one. There are seven—one for each day:

Monday. "A person's days are determined; you have decreed the number of his months and have set limits he cannot exceed. So look away from him and let him alone till he has put in his time like a hired laborer" (Job 14:5–6). "You have taken from me friend and neighbor—[now] darkness is my closest friend" (Psalm 88:18). *What does it say that God not only allows, even includes, such thoughts in His Word? He knows how we feel and speak when we are desperate.*[4]

Tuesday. "The righteous perish, and no one takes it to heart; the devout are taken away, and no one understands that the righteous are taken away to be spared from evil. Those who walk uprightly enter into peace; they find rest as they lie in death" (Isaiah 57:1, 2). *From our perspective, death—especially for the young—is nothing but a great evil. Yet we don't know the future, and what if death is God's way of taking people to himself, giving them peace, and saving them from evil. Why is this so counterintuitive for human beings?*

Wednesday. Read John 11:17–44. Jesus shows that he sees death from both the perspective of God and from the viewpoint of the bereaved human beings. He weeps with Mary and Martha, yet is moved with anger (verse 38) toward death, even knowing that he will immediately raise Lazarus to life. *Even if God is bringing His people home to Himself, He knows the sorrow and devastation death creates, and grieves with us. Does knowing that God hates death help you in any way?* "Jesus said to her, 'I am the resurrection and the life. The one who believes in me will live, even though they die; and whoever lives by believing in me will never die. Do you believe this?'" (John 11:25–26). *Do you believe this? If you do, how should that affect how you grieve?*

Thursday. "And if Christ has not been raised, your faith is futile; you are still in your sins. Then those also who have fallen asleep in Christ are lost. If only for this life we have hope in Christ, we are of all people most to be pitied. But Christ has indeed been raised from the dead, the firstfruits of those who have fallen asleep. For since death came through a man, the resurrection of the dead comes also through a man. For as in Adam all die, so in Christ all will be made alive" (1 Corinthians 15:17–22). *Paul is staking the credibility of all of Christianity on whether Jesus was raised from the dead or not. If Christian belief is merely a comfort in this life, then we are to be pitied, and those who have died hoping in Christ are gone forever. So before any other of the teaching or claims of Christianity are considered, this is the primary question: Was Jesus raised from the dead? If the answer is yes, then the way forward, though painful, leads to hope. If no, then life is meaningless. Which is it?*

Friday. "For we know that if the earthly tent we live in is destroyed, we have a building from God, an eternal house in heaven, not built by human hands. Meanwhile we groan, longing to be clothed instead with our heavenly dwelling, because when we are clothed, we will not be found naked. For while we are in this tent, we groan and are burdened, because we do not wish to be unclothed but to be clothed instead with our heavenly dwelling, so that what is mortal may be swallowed up by life. Now the one who has fashioned us for this very purpose is God, who has given us the Spirit as a deposit, guaranteeing what is to come" (2 Corinthians 5:1–5). *Paul is specifically rejecting the idea that when we die we become disembodied spirits; instead, we are further clothed, with immortality. This was a theme he had also treated in 1 Corinthians 15, when he talked about the resurrection of the body (verses 42–54). So passing through death is not entering a nebulous, ghostly afterlife, but a life of unimaginable fullness and joy. Our loved ones do not leave us and go into the dark. They leave us and go into the Light.*

Saturday. "The LORD is my shepherd; I shall not want. He makes me lie down in green pastures. He leads me beside still waters. He restores my soul. He leads me in paths of righteousness for his name's sake. Even though I walk through the valley of the shadow of death, I will fear no evil, for you are with me; your rod and your staff, they comfort me. You prepare a table before me in the presence of my enemies; you anoint my head with oil; my cup overflows. Surely goodness and mercy shall follow me all the days of my life and I shall dwell in the house of the LORD forever" (Psalm 23, ESV). *Here is a whole set of comforts for those who grieve. Remember that when you walk into the valley of the shadow of death, it is Jesus, the Shepherd, who has led you there. He has comfort to give you and ways to strengthen, deepen, and grow you that would be otherwise impossible. So give thanks for his presence, refuse self-pity, and seek him in prayer even when you don't feel him present (because he is). Jesus himself walked into death, solitary and rejected by everyone (Matthew 27:46), so when we face the death of loved ones or even our own death, we will never be alone.*

Sunday. "Therefore, there is now no condemnation for those who are in Christ Jesus, because through Christ Jesus the law of the Spirit who gives life has set you free from the law of sin and death" (Romans 8:1–2). *Many people are unaware of the condemnation that has been pronounced over them, or else they are unacquainted with its magnitude, except perhaps for a nagging sense of unease. When facing death, however, our enemy allows us to see the full scope of our cosmic treason, and what answer do we have then? Only this—that Jesus has taken our punishment and set us free, and there is now no condemnation left for us. Rejoice!*

Acknowledgments

As ever, thanks to our editor at Viking, Brian Tart. It was Brian who saw the short meditation on death that I preached at Terry Hall's funeral and proposed that we turn it not only into one but three short books on birth, marriage, and death. We also thank our many friends in South Carolina who made it possible to write this and the companion books while at Folly Beach last summer. Finally and most significantly, I want to thank my wife, Kathy, who did endless iterations of editing to turn my original sermon from the funeral of her sister, Terry Hall, into this short book. Kathy was very much a coauthor. Thanks, honey.

Notes

Foreword

1. From the famous quote by Samuel Johnson, found in James Boswell, *The Life of Samuel Johnson, LLD* (New York: Penguin Classics, 2008), 231.

The Fear of Death: Conscience Makes Cowards of Us All

1. William Shakespeare, *Hamlet*, 4.3.30–31: "A man may fish with the worm that hath eat of a king."
2. Ernest Becker, *The Denial of Death* (New York: The Free Press, 1973), 26.
3. Annie Dillard, *The Living: A Novel* (New York: HarperCollins, 1992), 141.
4. Howard P. Chudacoff, *Children at Play: An American History* (New York: New York University Press, 2007), 22.

5. Atul Gawande, *Being Mortal: Medicine and What Matters in the End* (New York: Metropolitan Books, 2014).

6. Geoffrey Gorer, "The Pornography of Death," 2003. This article may be found at www .romolocapuano.com/wp-content/uploads /2013/08/Gorer.pdf.

7. See David Bosworth, "The New Immortalists," *Hedgehog Review* 17, no. 2 (Summer 2015).

8. Richard A. Shweder, Nancy C. Much, Manamohan Mahapatra, and Lawrence Park, "The 'Big Three' of Morality (Autonomy, Community, Divinity) and the 'Big Three' Explanations of Suffering," in Richard A. Shweder, *Why Do Men Barbecue? Recipes for Cultural Psychology* (Cambridge, MA: Harvard University Press, 2003), 74. For more on this subject, see "The Cultures of Suffering" in Timothy Keller, *Walking with God through Pain and Suffering* (New York: Penguin/ Riverhead, 2013), 13–34.

9. Shweder, *Why Do Men Barbecue? Recipes for Cultural Psychology*, 125.

10. Mark Ashton, *On My Way to Heaven: Facing Death with Christ* (Chorley, UK: 10Publishing, 2010), 7–8.

11. Becker, *The Denial of Death*, xvii.

12. Becker, *The Denial of Death*, xvii.

13. Albert Camus, *The Myth of Sisyphus and Other Essays* (New York: Alfred A. Knopf, 1955).

14. Becker, *The Denial of Death*, 26–27.

15. See Julian Barnes, *Nothing to Be Frightened Of* (London: Jonathan Cape, 2008). The article by Jessica E. Brown, "We Fear Death, but What If Dying Isn't as Bad as We Think?," is from *The Guardian*, July 25, 2017.

16. Luc Ferry, *A Brief History of Thought: A Philosophical Guide to Living* (New York: Harper, 2010), 4.

17. From Dylan Thomas, *In Country Sleep, and Other Poems* (London: Dent, 1952). The poem can be found at www.poets.org/poetsorg /poem/do-not-go-gentle-good-night.

18. Quoted in Wilfred M. McClay, "The Strange Persistence of Guilt," *Hedgehog Review* 19, no. 1 (Spring 2017).

19. McClay, "The Strange Persistence of Guilt."

20. McClay, "The Strange Persistence of Guilt."

21. Andrew Delbanco, *The Death of Satan: How Americans Have Lost the Sense of Evil* (New York: Farrar, Straus and Giroux, 1995), 3, 9.

22. David Brooks, "The Cruelty of Call-Out Culture," *New York Times*, January 14, 2019.

23. McClay, "The Strange Persistence of Guilt."
24. From Eliot, "Murder in the Cathedral," in *The Complete Plays of T. S. Eliot* (New York: Harcourt, Brace, and World, Inc., 1935), 43.
25. *Hamlet*, 3.1.87–88, 91.
26. This story was related by Dr. Leitch to a group of college students, of which I was one, at Bucknell University in 1970.
27. William L. Lane, Word Biblical Commentary *Hebrews 1–8*, vol. 47, (Dallas, TX: Word Books, 1991), 55–58.
28. C. S. Lewis, "The Weight of Glory," is found at www.newcityindy.org/wp-content/uploads/2012/06/Lewis-Weight-of-Glory.pdf.
29. Margaret N. Barnhouse, *That Man Barnhouse* (Carol Stream, IL: Tyndale House, 1983), 186.

The Rupture of Death:
Do Not Grieve Like Those Without Hope

1. See any commentary. One example: George R. Beasley-Murray, *John*, vol. 36, Word Biblical Commentary (Plano, TX: Thomas Nelson, 1999), 194.
2. Homer, *The Iliad*, 24.549–51, quoted in N. T.

Wright, *The Resurrection of the Son of God* (Minneapolis, MN: Fortress Press, 2003), 2.

3. Peter Kreeft, *Love Is Stronger Than Death* (San Francisco: Ignatius Press, 1979), 2–3.

4. See Jonathan Edwards, "Sermon Fifteen: Heaven Is a World of Love," in *The Works of Jonathan Edwards*, WJE Online, Jonathan Edwards Center, Yale University, edwards .yale.edu/archive?path=aHR0cDovL2Vkd2Fy ZHMueWFsZS5lZHUvY2dpLWJpbi9uZXd waGlsby9nZXRvYmplY3QucGw/Yy43O jQ6MTUud2plbw==.

5. From the hymn "Sometimes a Light Surprises," William Cowper, 1779.

6. C. S. Lewis, "The Weight of Glory," is found at www.newcityindy.org/wp-content/uploads /2012/06/Lewis-Weight-of-Glory.pdf.

7. John Flavel, *Pneumatologia: A Treatise of the Soul of Man.* In *The Works of John Flavel*, vol. 3 (Edinburgh: Banner of Truth Trust, 1968), 121. Some of the language is modernized.

8. Cited in F. F. Bruce, *1 and 2 Thessalonians*, vol. 45, Word Biblical Commentary (Plano, TX: Thomas Nelson, 1982), 96.

9. For example, see N. T. Wright, *Resurrection of the Son of God*, 32–206.

10. C. S. Lewis, *Mere Christianity* (New York: Macmillan, 1960), 174–75.

Appendix

1. From "How Firm a Foundation," a hymn by John Rippon, 1787.
2. C. S. Lewis, *A Grief Observed* (New York: HarperOne, 2001), 63, 76.
3. From "Crown Him with Many Crowns," a hymn by Matthew Bridges and Godfrey Thring, 1851.
4. Derek Kidner, *Psalms 1–72: An Introduction and Commentary* (Leicester, UK: Inter-Varsity Press, 1973), 157.

Further Reading

Joseph Bayly. *The View from a Hearse*. Elgin, IL.: David C. Cook, 1969.

Elisabeth Elliot. *Facing the Death of Someone You Love*. Westchester, IL.: Good News Publishers, 1982.

Timothy Keller. *Walking with God Through Pain and Suffering*. New York: Penguin/Riverhead, 2013.

Timothy Keller. *Making Sense of God: Finding God in the Modern World*. New York: Penguin, 2016.

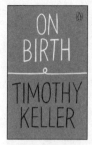
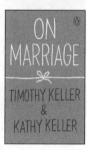

PENGUIN BOOKS

ON MARRIAGE

Timothy Keller started Redeemer Presbyterian Church in New York City with his wife, Kathy, and their three sons. Redeemer grew to nearly 5,500 regular Sunday attendees and helped to start more than three hundred new churches around the world. In 2017 Keller moved from his role as senior minister at Redeemer to the staff of Redeemer City to City, an organization that helps national church leaders around the world reach and minister in global cities. He is the author of *The Prodigal Prophet*, *God's Wisdom for Navigating Life*, as well as *The Meaning of Marriage*, *The Prodigal God*, and *The Reason for God*, among others.

Kathy Keller received her MA in theological studies at Gordon-Conwell Theological Seminary. Kathy and Tim then moved to Virginia, where Tim started at his first church, West Hopewell Presbyterian Church. After nine years, Kathy and her family moved to New York City to start the Redeemer Presbyterian Church. Kathy cowrote *The Meaning of Marriage*, *The Songs of Jesus*, *God's Wisdom for Navigating Life*, and *The Meaning of Marriage: A Couple's Devotional* with Tim. *On Marriage* is their fifth collaboration.

ALSO BY THE AUTHORS

The Meaning of Marriage
The Songs of Jesus
God's Wisdom for Navigating Life
The Meaning of Marriage: A Couple's Devotional

ALSO BY TIMOTHY KELLER

The Reason for God
The Prodigal God
Counterfeit Gods
Generous Justice
Jesus the King
Center Church
Every Good Endeavor
Walking with God through Pain and Suffering
Encounters with Jesus
Prayer
Preaching
Making Sense of God
Hidden Christmas
The Prodigal Prophet
On Birth
On Death

On Marriage

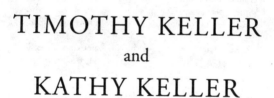

TIMOTHY KELLER
and
KATHY KELLER

PENGUIN BOOKS

PENGUIN BOOKS
An imprint of Penguin Random House LLC
penguinrandomhouse.com

Copyright © 2020 by Timothy Keller and Kathy Keller
Penguin supports copyright. Copyright fuels creativity,
encourages diverse voices, promotes free speech, and creates a
vibrant culture. Thank you for buying an authorized edition
of this book and for complying with copyright laws by not
reproducing, scanning, or distributing any part of it in any form
without permission. You are supporting writers and allowing
Penguin to continue to publish books for every reader.

All Bible references are from the New International Version
(NIV), unless otherwise noted.

ISBN 9780143135364 (paperback)
ISBN 9780525507024 (ebook)

Printed in the United States of America
1   3   5   7   9   10   8   6   4   2

Set in Adobe Garamond   ·   Designed by Sabrina Bowers

*In memory of Dr. R. C. Sproul, who performed our
wedding and got both our theology and our
marriage going in the right direction*

Contents

Introduction to the
How to Find God Series · *xi*

Beginning a Marriage · *1*

Sustaining a Marriage · *43*

The Destiny of Marriage · *75*

Acknowledgments · *99*

Notes · *101*

Introduction to the How to Find God Series

Life is a journey, and finding and knowing God is fundamental to that journey. When a new child is born, when we approach marriage, and when we find ourselves facing death—either in old age or much earlier—it tends to concentrate the mind. We shake ourselves temporarily free from absorption in the whirl of daily life and ask the big questions of the ages:

Am I living for things that matter?

Will I have what it takes to face this new stage of life?

Do I have a real relationship with God?

The most fundamental transition any human being can make is what the Bible refers to as the new birth (John 3:1–8), or becoming a "new creation" (2 Corinthians 5:17). This can happen at any time in a life, of course, but often the circumstances that lead us to vital faith in Christ occur during these tectonic shifts in life stages. Over forty-five years of ministry, my wife, Kathy, and I have seen that people are particularly open to exploring a relationship with God at times of major life transition.

In this series of short books we want to help readers facing major life changes to think about

what constitutes the truly changed life. Our purpose is to give readers the Christian foundations for life's most important and profound moments. We start with birth and baptism, move into marriage, and conclude with death. Our hope is that these slim books will provide guidance, comfort, wisdom, and, above all, will help point the way to finding and knowing God all throughout your life.

On Marriage

Beginning
a Marriage

Why bother to get married at all?

In the words of the traditional Christian wedding service, "God has established and sanctified marriage for the welfare and happiness of humankind."[1] While true, that cannot be the end of the discussion for modern people.

This is a more pressing question now than it has ever been in previous times. In the past it was a given that to become an adult member of society you married and had children, and the vast majority of people did so. But younger adults in Western countries today postpone marriage at unprecedented rates. Nearly a third of all millennials in the United States may stay unmarried through age forty, and 25 percent may not marry at all, the highest proportion of any generation in modern history.[2] Why? There are two reasons that so many marriages never begin: economic stress and the rise of individualism in culture.

Fears About Marriage

The economic factor is seen in the widespread belief of single adults that they must be financially secure in a good career before they marry and that, of course, their prospective mate should be as well. The background assumption is that married life is a drain on resources, especially with the arrival of children. Before marrying, it is therefore believed, you should have a guaranteed income stream, adequate savings, and perhaps even an investment portfolio.

However, this view flies in the face of both statistics and tradition. Traditionally, you got married not because you were economically secure and stable, but in order to become so. Marriage brings with it unique economic benefits. Studies show that married couples save significantly more than singles. Spouses can encourage one another to greater levels of self-discipline than can friends. Spouses also provide each other with more support through the trials of life, so that they experience greater physical and mental health than singles.

The other factor in the decline of marriage to which experts point is "expressive individ-

ualism."³ This is a term popularized by soci-
ologists to describe a growing cultural trend.
In traditional cultures our personal identity was
worked out in our relationships. "Who I am"
was defined by my place in a family and community, and perhaps by my place in the universe with God. I became a person of worth
as I fulfilled my responsibilities in these relationships. In modern times, however, we have
turned inward. "Who I am" must not be determined by what anyone else says or thinks
about me. I become a person of worth as I
discover my own deepest desires and feelings
and express them. Once I determine who I am,
then I can enter into relationships, but only
with those who accept me on my own terms.

This modern approach to identity is instilled in us by our culture in countless ways.

In the 2016 film *Moana*, the crown princess of a Polynesian island has been told by her father that she is the island's future leader and will have to submit to many traditional responsibilities. But instead, Moana has a desire to set out to sea to find adventure. Her grandmother sings her a song that tells her that her "true self" resides not in her duties and social responsibilities, but in the expression of her inmost desires. She tells Moana that if a "voice inside" her heart tells her to follow her desires, "that voice inside is *who you are*."[4]

We are assailed by this message at every turn—in television, movies, advertising, classrooms, books, social media, and casual conversation—until it is an unquestioned, virtually invisible assumption about how we become authentic persons.

The effect of this modern self on marriage has been considerable. It means that we do not want to even consider marriage if we have not established our own unique identity. We don't want anyone else to have any say in who we are until we have fully decided it for ourselves. Further, today we expect and even demand that all relationships be transactional, provisional as long as profitable, and never binding and permanent. If impermanence is the standard, then marriage and particularly parenting are deeply problematic since leaving a marriage is difficult and leaving a parenting relationship is essentially impossible. What if a relationship with a spouse or a child gets in the way of your expressing your "true self"?

Many modern people only marry if they believe they have found a spouse who won't try to change them and who will provide emotional and financial resources to help them toward their personal goals.

But it is an illusion to think that we find ourselves only by looking inside, rather than in relationships with those outside of us. In every heart there are deep, multiple, contradictory desires. Fear and anger exist alongside hope and aspiration. We try to sort these contradictory desires, determining which ones are "not really me." But what if they are *all* a part of me? How do we make decisions about which are "us" and which are not?

The answer is that we come to admire and respect some individuals or groups whose views we then deploy to sift and assess the impulses of our hearts. In other words, contrary to what we are told, we *do* develop an identity not merely by looking inside but through important relationships and narratives that profoundly shape how we see ourselves. We do *not* merely look within.

The traditional approach to marriage was wise, in that people knew intuitively that it would profoundly shape and reshape our identity. And that's good—because identity is always worked out in negotiation with significant others in your life. As psychologist Jennifer B. Rhodes put it, "In previous generations people were more willing to make that decision [to marry] and [then] figure it out."[5] What better way to discover who you are than to marry someone you love and respect, and then figure it out together?

So the contemporary decline in marriage is based on two mistaken beliefs about it, namely, that it is a drain economically and it is an impediment to the full realization of our freedom and identity.

Marriage Was Made for Us

Social scientists have marshaled evidence against these two mistaken views, showing how significantly marriage benefits us both economically and psychologically. In addition, they have demonstrated how crucial the traditional family is to the welfare of the young, that children do much better if raised in families of two married parents. But Christians should not be at all surprised by these findings.[6] The book of Genesis tells us that God established marriage even as he created the human race. This should not be understood to teach that every individual adult must be married. Jesus himself was single, and since he stands as the great exemplar of what a human being should be, we cannot insist—as some cultures have—that you must be married to be a fully realized person. But neither can we see marriage, as our own culture does, as merely a development to guard property rights during the Neolithic Age that today can be altered or discarded as we please.

Wendell Berry famously addressed the modern idea that whether we have sex inside marriage or outside is "a completely private decision." He disagreed, saying, "Sex is not and cannot be any individual's 'own business,' nor is it merely the private concern of any couple. Sex, like any other necessary, precious, and volatile power that is commonly held, is everybody's business."[7] Sex outside of marriage creates babies outside of marriages, it often spreads disease, and it habituates us to treat others as pleasure objects rather than persons. All of these have a major impact on social conditions, conditions that affect everyone.

We know this line of thinking is deeply counterintuitive to modern people in the West, but it has been quite natural to most human beings in most places and times. Your choice regarding marriage is not ultimately a private decision. It affects everyone around you.

Marriage was made for us, and the human race was made for marriage.

Fear of Failure

There is another reason many people give to explain the modern reticence to marry. "I saw how difficult my own parents' marriage was, and I don't want that for myself." A fear of strife and marital failure keeps many people from seeking a spouse or, at least, makes them look for a prospective mate with virtually no flaws or personal weaknesses. Some people assume that if their parents divorced, their own future marriage is much more likely to end in divorce.

Joe Pinsker, in an article in *The Atlantic*, argues that not only does recent research show this is not true, but exposure to bad marriages can give you the resources to build a good one.[8] He gives the example of a man named Justin Lange. After his parents' divorce, Justin saw his mother remarry twice and his father three more times. He concluded that marriage was simply too hard and that he would never enter into it. But he met a woman, fell in love, and is now happily married after all. Why? "He attributes his present happiness . . . to going *against* the example his parents set."[9] He learned how to build a good marriage by *not* doing what they had done wrong.

Above all, he recognized his parents' biggest failure—to verbally make a lifetime commitment and then "not be willing to back it up." Divorce is sometimes necessary and the Bible allows for it. But longitudinal studies show that two-thirds of unhappy marriages, if they continue, become happy within five years.[10] Lange learned it was an illusion to believe that if he found the right partner they wouldn't fight like their parents did. He overcame the fear that marriage would be difficult. Of course it would be. He also overcame his fear that there would be fights. Of course there would be. But the secret is not to let these things weaken your commitment to love each other through it all. He said, "You may be upset about whatever mundane thing it is today, but is it going to matter later on? Just let it roll and focus on the important things."[11]

Misunderstanding Sex

There is another reason often given by both researchers as well as men themselves why males are less interested in marriage than in the past. Researchers point out that the ready availability of sex is one reason for the decline in marriage.[12] We have often heard men tell us the same thing directly: "It used to be that you pretty much had to get married to have a sexual relationship, but that's changed completely."

This attitude views sex as a commodity that used to be expensive. At one time you had to give up your independence through marriage in order to get sex. It was costly, but now it is available more cheaply, as it were. All such talk, however, conceives of sex as a physical and emotional experience that can be just as good if not better outside of marriage as it is inside.

From its very beginning, Christianity brought a revolutionary new understanding of sex into the world. It was seen as just one part—one uniquely joyful, powerful, and inseparable part—of mutual self-giving. To be loved and admired but not truly known is only mildly satisfying. To be known but rejected and not loved is our greatest nightmare. But to become vulnerable and so fully known and yet accepted and fully loved by someone we admire—that is the greatest possible satisfaction. In marriage, spouses lose their independence and so become vulnerable and interdependent. They do not hold themselves back so that they only relate temporarily, provisionally, and transactionally. They give their entire selves to each other—emotionally, physically, legally, economically.

The startling sex ethic of the early Christians was that sex is both a sign and a means for that total self-giving, and that it must not be used for any other purpose. To engage in sex for any other reason was to misunderstand it. Granting access to our physical bodies must be accompanied by the opening of our whole lives to each other through a life-long marriage covenant. Only in that situation, the early Christians taught, does sex become the unitive and fulfilling act it was meant to be.

This new sexual code of "no sex outside of marriage" startled the Roman world because it seemed highly restrictive.[13] But it actually elevated sex from a mere commodity of pleasure into a way to create the deepest possible bond and community between two human beings, as well as a way to honor and resemble the One who gave himself wholly for us so we could be liberated to give ourselves exclusively to him.

Flee from sexual immorality . . . Do you not know that your bodies are temples of the Holy Spirit, who is in you, whom you have received from God? You are not your own; you were bought at a price. Therefore honor God with your bodies. (1 Corinthians 6:18–20)

Like the citizens of ancient Rome, modern people see the biblical sex ethic as restrictive and unattractive. And yet there are signs and evidences that the supposed outdated Christian view still resonates with our deeper intuitions about sex.

Superconsensual Sex

A woman writing in *The New York Times* described a sexual encounter with a man she had met on Tinder. She was nearly thirty and he was twenty-four, an age difference that did not seem significant until he began "asking for my consent about nearly everything."[14] He asked if he could take her sweater off and after she said yes he also asked if he could take off her tank top, then her bra. She snorted that he didn't have to ask permission for every little thing. "A dramatic shift" had taken place in the "sexual training" of younger men, leading them to repeatedly ask for verbal consent. After it was all over, she said, "In fact I had liked it as a form of care-taking. I just wasn't used to being taken care of in that way."[15] It had felt very intimate.

Later, however, when she texted him, he did not answer; he simply "ghosted" her. When she told her roommates how hurt she was, they couldn't understand. "Because he

asked for my consent, over and over," she explained, "sex felt like a sacred act, and then he
disappeared." They didn't understand why she
was so hurt but,

> . . . in the days and weeks after, I was
> left thinking that our culture's current
> approach to consent is too narrow . . .
> Consent doesn't work if we relegate it
> exclusively to the sexual realm. Our
> bodies are only one part of the com-
> plex constellation of who we are. To
> base our culture of consent on the
> body alone is to expect that caretak-
> ing involves only the physical. I wish
> we could view consent as something
> that's . . . more about care for the
> other person, the entire person . . .

Because I don't think many of us would say yes to the question "Is it O.K. if I act like I care about you and then disappear?"[16]

If what the Bible says about God's design for marriage and sexuality is true, then this woman's experience is not surprising. Giving our bodies to each other without giving our whole lives fails to recognize the integrated nature of the self. The body can't be separated from the whole. Sex should indeed be a reciprocal offering of each other's lives, and to give your body to someone who feels free to leave afterward and not care for you is dehumanizing.

Christians have the deepest and broadest understanding of consent possible. When

Christians say that sex is for marriage only, they mean sex must be superconsensual.

Seeking Marriage Well

So how do you begin a marriage? Most readers would answer: by seeking and finding someone to marry, obviously. But that answer is a modern one. In past times spouses were provided to you by families. Even a hundred years ago, although you made your own choices, your options were limited. Most people lived in smaller communities. You had to select a spouse from a fairly small pool of people, and virtually all of them could be evaluated over years, through face-to-face interaction.

All that has changed. Now if you go on dating apps such as OkCupid, you join 30 mil-

lion other users. The number of potential partners is dizzying and the challenge of choosing
among them can be paralyzing. Even if you
get over your fear, however, the very mode
of evaluating thousands of people not by face-
to-face experience but online can reshape marriage seeking into a shopping experience.
Persons are reduced to consumer products as
you compare their height, weight, looks, and
so on.

The problem is that even without social
media we were always too prone to operating
in this way. It is instinctive for a single person
to walk into a room of other singles and to
implicitly eliminate as prospective partners anyone who does not make the cut on the basis
of physical and financial factors. Once we
have eliminated them, we take a second look
at those left in our pool and evaluate for

things like character and a feeling of "connection" or affinity. The problem is that you have already ruled out people who may have the character and affinity you seek.

Social media and dating apps only accentuate this self-defeating strategy many times over. One major problem is that the people you are looking at online are providing you a highly filtered representation. You are looking for character and connection, but as one researcher points out: "There is no evidence that you can assess that online." Instead, says Eli Finkel of Northwestern University, online misconceptions are rampant. "You think you know what you want but what you really need is to sit across from each other and get a beer."[17]

Does this mean you should not try to meet

people online? Not necessarily, but the only way to proceed is to, first, resist the "shopping experience" approach to marriage seeking that eliminates people based purely on the physical and financial and, second, find ways to "sit across from each other" and get to know them.

Once we find ways to sit across from someone, what are we looking for?

1. *Look for another believer, if you are a Christian.*

At first glance this seems like a statement of prejudice, but if someone does not share your Christian faith that means that he or she does not understand it. And, if your faith is at all important to how you think and live, it means they don't understand you either. Surely the essence of a good marriage is someone who "gets" you, but if someone doesn't share your faith, they can't. The only way to let such a relationship grow in intimacy is if you make Jesus more peripheral in your daily thinking and feeling.

2 Corinthians 6:14 urges Christians not to be "unequally yoked" in our closest relationships with people who don't share our deepest beliefs. The image is of a farmer trying to yoke together two different animals—say an ox and a donkey—who were of different heights, weights, and gaits. The heavy wooden yoke, instead of harnessing the power of the team to do the task, would rub and chafe *both* animals. So a marriage between someone who is a practicing, believing Christian and someone who is not can be unfair and painful to both partners.

2. Look for someone who will still attract you when they lose their youthful looks.

While physical attraction must grow between married partners, it should be based on a deeper sort of attraction. In the Bible book Song of Solomon, the lover says, "You have stolen my heart with one glance of your eyes" (Song of Solomon 4:9). As much as this book of the Bible rejoices in sexual love, the part of the body that gets the most attention from the lovers is the other person's eyes. And this is not so much a focus on the loveliness of their physical shape; the "glance" of the eyes reveals the character and personality of the lover. Indeed, when bodies are aging and losing their loveliness, the glance of the eyes can be even more thoughtful and wise, more joyful and loving. To be captivated by someone's eyes is a way of saying you are attracted to the person's heart.

Romantic attraction should not ignore physical looks, but it must not be the most important part, because no one keeps their looks over the long haul. Paul tells us in 2 Corinthians 4:16 that even as their bodies become weaker and older, believers can be growing stronger and more beautiful internally. The more we fix our gaze on the loveliness of our partner's inward being, the more our physical attraction will grow even as our physical attractiveness lessens over the years.

3. *Finally, get advice from others about your relationship before you proceed to marriage.*

In the past it was unlikely that you would enter into a romance with someone your family and friends didn't know. Feedback about your partner came naturally from many people who knew you as well as him or her. Today we are mobile people living on our mobile phones. We move from place to place. Many who actually see us in person every day are people who don't know us well. Meanwhile many of the people who have known us the longest are distant and can only "see" us through filtered representations online. Many of our most longtime associates are in the dark about how we are really doing.

The result is that we make more decisions in a vacuum, including decisions about romance and marriage. But marriage is too important a choice to be made without counsel, and there are married couples with the accumulated wisdom and experience from whom you need to hear. Take advantage of this wisdom and seek advice from the married couples in your life.

Starting Marriage Well

Once you marry, how do you begin to lay the foundation for a long, rich marriage?

In advance of our marriage Kathy was told numerous times that her wedding day would be "the happiest day of her life." We sincerely hoped not! Every day following the wedding has been a day in which we moved forward in understanding each other and in adjusting to and serving each other. Every day has been one more day to learn and enjoy better the fruits of repentance and forgiveness.

Our attitude might have had something to do with an offhand comment by R. C.

Sproul, the minister who performed our marriage service. He said, "Vesta and I have been married for fifteen years now, and we think we're just about getting the hang of it." At first glance that might seem like an intimidating statement—fifteen years of marriage and they were *still* just getting the hang of it? But now, from the vantage point of our forty-five years of marriage, we are inclined to think he underestimated how long it takes to learn each other's heart and life rhythms, to practice self-denial in the service of the health of the relationship, and to grow in the knowledge of alien (someone else's) love languages. But whether the learning curve is long or short, any marriage must begin well in order to be built better. We have considered a few (not the only) important foundational habits, practices, behaviors, and attitudes that should be established at the outset.[18]

1. ***Never go to bed angry.*** It's become a cliché, but there is a strong biblical reason behind it. This follows Saint Paul's direction to "not let the sun go down on your anger" in Ephesians 4:26. That means that rather than repress and hide your unhappiness, you and your spouse must become adept at a new skill set. Those skills include: First, you must express what is bothering you in a way that is truthful but not an attack. Second, you must learn to sincerely repent for how you've hurt your spouse but do so by neither excusing yourself nor engaging in so much self-shaming that your spouse just says, "Forget I brought it up." Third, you must learn how to give and to receive forgiveness.

In medical circles it is widely believed that

sleep is the time when what is learned and experienced during the day becomes organized into memories and habits. If you go to bed angry at your spouse, you will nourish an attitude of resentment. If you do it enough times, it will grow into a deeply felt anger, even hatred. How does one avoid going to bed angry? See number 2.

2. *Pray together as your last words of the day.* One can hardly pray in anger (not very easily, anyway), and even if all you do is spend five minutes petitioning God for his blessing on your family and your lives, you will have to relinquish your anger in order to enter God's presence.

3. *Give each other sex often.* This would seem like a no-brainer to newlyweds! However,

sexual energy is like all other energy, and when you are tired it is easy to forget or put off sex for "a better time." Lack of intimate touching can lead to distance between spouses. We use the word "give" intentionally. All of us have fallen into the myth that wild flights of passion possess each partner simultaneously, when the truth is that usually one person is more interested in sex than the other. On those occasions, the less-interested spouse can *give* sex as a gift. Saint Paul, himself a bachelor, makes this into a culture-challenging biblical command:

> The husband should fulfill his marital
> duty to his wife, and likewise the wife
> to her husband. The wife does not

have authority over her own body but yields it to her husband. In the same way, the husband does not have authority over his own body but yields it to his wife. Do not deprive each other except perhaps by mutual consent and for a time, so that you may devote yourselves to prayer. Then come together again so that Satan will not tempt you because of your lack of self-control. (1 Corinthians 7:3–5)

In a world where men had all the sexual privileges, Paul insists that husbands and wives have equal rights over each other's bodies, and that it is not a good thing to "deprive" each other unless it is by mutual consent, and then for only a short period.

4. ***Make deliberate decisions about your
   family life and traditions.*** You will have
   grown up observing your parents or other
   adults in their roles as men and women,
   husband and wife, parents, grandparents,
   and so on. You will have no choice but to
   unconsciously carry those prototypes with
   you into your own marriage. *That* is how a
   husband treats his wife. *This* is the way we
   celebrate holidays. Vacations *always* mean
   going to the beach. These assumptions will
   affect your life together in the big things
   and in the small, so it is best to make them
   conscious, examine them, and decide as a
   couple how your new family unit will do
   things.

When we got married, Kathy brought
with her the image of a father who cooked

Saturday breakfast so his wife could sleep in, and who could change a diaper with the best of them. (With five children he had gotten plenty of practice!) Tim, on the other hand, had lived in a family where his father had to be at work at 5:00 A.M., returning exhausted in the evening. Beyond providing for his family, he was not asked to contribute in any way. Shortly after our first son was born, Tim's parents took him aside, worried that he was being "henpecked" because Kathy had asked him to change a diaper. He firmly said, "Mom and Dad, thanks for your concern, but in our family we do things differently than you did." Opening gifts on Christmas Eve or Christmas morning? You decide together. Music or TV turned on first thing in the morning, or not? (Kathy let out a screech when Tim turned on the radio the first morning we awoke in our apartment to-gether! Should have discussed that one!)

We are not discussing the odious practice of negotiating every chore and keeping score to see who fulfills their bargain. We have talked about male and female roles in marriage at length elsewhere. We're talking about creating new traditions that fit your new family, rather than making assumptions about how things are done based on your family of origin.

5. Finally, *learn each other's "love languages."* One of the most important books we ever read was Judson Swihart's *How Do You Say "I Love You"?*[19] Early in the book he gives an illustration of a German-speaking man saying *"Ich liebe*

dich" to a girl who speaks only French. He is loving her but she doesn't feel the love because he is literally not conveying it in a language she can understand. That's natural, he writes, because "most people only speak those languages they themselves understand."[20]

He goes on to argue—quite rightly, in our experience—that each of us has certain ways we want love expressed to us. In our premarital counseling, R. C. told this story from his own marriage as an illustration. For his birthday he was hoping for a new set of golf clubs, something he would not have bought for himself. However, his practical wife, Vesta, got him six new white shirts. When her birthday came around he surprised her with a fancy new coat, sure she would be delighted, but what she really wanted was a new washing machine. They had missed each other's love language, speaking only their own.

For us, when Tim proactively helps Kathy with her domestic duties around the house, that is much more emotionally valuable to her than when he verbally says how much he loves her, or even when he buys her a gift. In other words, when he "says" he loves her in that way she feels much more loved than if he expresses it some other way. He's speaking her language. Swihart and others give you a whole list of "love languages": spending time together, meeting emotional needs, saying it with words, saying it with touch, being on the same side, bringing out the best in each other, and others. It is crucial to discover your spouse's most valued languages and become fluent in them even if they are not similarly important to you.

Discuss, agree, and begin to do these five things, and your marriage is off and running!

Sustaining a Marriage

The Bible begins with a marriage in Genesis and ends with a marriage at the wedding supper of the Lamb in Revelation. The Christian understanding is that marriage points us to God and the gospel— but at the same time it is the gospel that gives us the greatest possible resources for marriage. Here's the first marriage depicted for us in Genesis, chapter 2.

> The LORD God said, "It is not good for the man to be alone. I will make a

helper suitable for him." Now the LORD God had formed out of the ground all the beasts of the field and all the birds of the air. He brought them to the man to see what he would name them; and whatever the man called each living creature, that was its name. So the man gave names to all the livestock, the birds of the air and all the beasts of the field. But for Adam no suitable helper was found. So the LORD God caused the man to fall into a deep sleep; and while he was sleeping, he took one of the man's ribs and closed up the place with flesh. Then the LORD God made a woman from the rib he had taken out of the man, and he brought her to the man. The man said, "This is now bone of my bones and flesh of my flesh; she shall be called 'woman,' for she was taken out of man." For this reason a man will leave his father and mother and is united to his wife, and they will become one flesh. The man and his wife were both naked, and they felt no shame. (Genesis 2:18–25)

Let's look at this passage to learn what we need for a good marriage over the long run, over decades. It speaks to us of three things we have to have.

Avoidance of Idolatry

It is customary in weddings for the bride to walk to the groom, often accompanied by her father or both parents or someone else. Genesis 2 shows us that the tradition stretches back to the garden of Eden. In this case it is God who is doing the honors, drawing the wife to the husband.

And when Adam sees Eve, he speaks poetry, the first recorded in the Bible. In most Bibles it is printed on the page indented and in verse form. The man explodes into song at the sight of his wife.

His first Hebrew word means "At last." It can also be translated "Finally!" He is saying, "This is what I've been looking for. This is what has been missing." But what is it? He says that she is "bone of my bones and flesh of my flesh." It's a way of saying "I have found myself in you. At last, by knowing you I can know myself." Remember that Adam is speaking from paradise, where he has a perfect relationship with God. Yet finding a spouse and partner speaks to something so profound in us that Adam erupts in adoration through artistic expression. This points to an important fact that we must understand if we are going to have a successful marriage over the long term.

John Newton, who is best known as the writer of the hymn "Amazing Grace," was also a wise pastor in eighteenth-century Britain. He wrote a series of letters to a young couple just starting out in marriage. He often counseled newlyweds, saying that you may think that having a bad marriage is the biggest problem you may face. However, a good marriage can be every bit as big a spiritual danger. He writes:

> With such an amiable partner, your
> chief danger perhaps will lie in being

too happy. Alas! the deceitfulness of our hearts, in a time of prosperity, exposes us to the greatest of evils, to wander from the fountain of living waters, and to sit down by broken cisterns. Permit me to hint to you, yea, to both of you: Beware of idolatry. I have smarted for it; it has distressed me with many imaginary fears, and cut me out much cause of real humiliation and grief. . . . The old leaven,— a tendency to the covenant of works, still cleaves to me.[1]

What is he talking about? He is using biblical imagery. Cisterns were open tanks made of stone or lime plaster that were used in ancient times to collect rainwater for use by people in their homes. But if the cistern was cracked, the water leaked out, leaving no remedy for thirst. "Broken cisterns" (Jeremiah 2:13) was a metaphor that the prophets used to describe how we look for our deepest satisfaction and security not in God, but in things of this world. Jesus told the woman in Samaria that the only source of final satisfaction was not in romance and marriage but in him (John 4:14), the source of "living water."

Newton is saying that good marriages run the great risk of turning your heart from God to your spouse as a greater source of love, safety, and joy. Not only that, Newton speaks of a good marriage as the cause of backsliding into a "covenant of works." What does that mean?

A "covenant of works" is an old theological term for a system in which you earn your salvation through your performance. You say to yourself, "The reason God will bless me and take me to heaven is that I'm living a good life and I deserve it." The Christian gospel is completely opposed to this mind-set. We are told, "For it is by grace you have been saved, through faith—and this is not from yourselves, it is the gift of God—not by [our good] works, so that no one can boast" (Ephesians 2:8–9).

John Newton as an Anglican minister knew this through and through, at least in his head. But, practically speaking, the idolization of his wife and marriage led him to slip back into a covenant of works. And that can happen to us. You will look to your spouse to give you the things only God can really give you. You can look to your spouse's love, your spouse's respect, your spouse's affirmation to give you a sense of your own value and worth. In other words, you will be looking to your spouse to save you. You are, in a sense, slipping back into the covenant of works.

This is easy to do because marriage is such a great thing. And it is easy to turn a great thing into the ultimate thing in your life.

As Newton says, it has led to many fears, humiliation, and grief. How? You put intolerable pressure on your spouse to always be healthy, happy, happy with you, and affirming. Yet nobody can bear the weight of that level of expectation. Criticism from your spouse can crush you. Problems with your spouse can devastate you, too. If anything at all goes wrong with your partner, your life may begin to collapse. And if your spouse dies, how can your "god" comfort you with love when he or she is in the coffin?

So what can we do? You must not try to lessen your love for your spouse or the person you think you're going to marry. Rather, you have to increase your love for God. C. S. Lewis says it is probably impossible to love any human being too much. You may love him too much in comparison to your love for God, but it is the smallness of your love for God, not the greatness of your love for the person, that constitutes the inordinacy. Marriage will ruin us unless we have a true and existential love relationship with God.[2]

Traditional societies believe you're nobody unless you're somebody's spouse, but the Christian faith was started by a single man. Saint Paul, in 2 Corinthians, says essentially, "You want to be married? Great. You're not married? Great." Paul means the relationship every single Christian has with God through Christ is so intimate and the relationship Christian brothers and sisters have inside the family of God can be so close, that no one who is single should be seen as having a life without family connections or as missing out on the greatest love of all.

So the first thing we need for a *great* marriage, paradoxically, is to see its penultimacy. But that's only the first thing we need.

Patience for the Long Journey

In Genesis 2:18 we read: "The LORD God said, 'It is not good for the man to be alone. I will make a helper suitable for him.'" The Hebrew word "*ezer*," translated as "helper," is regularly used in the Bible to refer to military reinforcements. Imagine you are a small troop overwhelmed by far greater enemy forces. Suddenly you see reinforcements rushing in to strengthen you in the battle. Think of your relief and joy! Without them you would have been defeated. That's the sense of the word here, and it is often used of God at places in the Bible. "Helper," then, does not mean "assistant," but rather someone who has a supplementary strength that you don't have. That is the word used for the woman, the wife in the first marriage relationship.

But there's another word—"suitable." Some have rendered this verse "I will make a helper *fit* for him." The King James translation famously has God saying, "I will make him an help *meet* for him." That's why "helpmeet" was a traditional (but now largely opaque) term for a wife.

Yet we should dig deeper for the full meaning of the original verse in Hebrew. Where the verse is translated as "I will make a helper suitable for him," there are actually two Hebrew words in the sentence that are translated by "suitable." The Hebrew literally says, "I will make a helper *like opposite* him." Our first impression is that this is a contradiction—is it "like" or is it "opposite"? But it clarifies things to think of two pieces of a puzzle. Two pieces of a puzzle fit together not if they are identical and not if they are randomly different. They only fit perfectly and form a whole if they are *rightly* different, different in a way that both corresponds yet complements.

God is sending into Adam's life (and therefore, God is also sending into Eve's life) someone with enormous power, but with a power that is different. "Like opposite," whatever else it means, means noninterchangeable. Each gender has excellencies and glories, perspectives and powers, that the other does not have. In marriage, a person of a different gender comes into your life—a person who is profoundly, mysteriously different.

Many people have tried to define masculinity and femininity with a list of specific characteristics. But as soon as you try to list them, you will find that they do not fit people in all cultures, nor even of all temperaments. Most important, the Bible does not give us a list of male and female traits. Yet gender differences are assumed in the Scripture, not least here in

Genesis 1 and 2. The message of the text is that only together, armed with the whole array of masculinity and femininity, are you going to be able to handle life as a married couple. The military background of the word "help" hints at this. Only together do you have what it takes not to be defeated.

We—Tim and Kathy—do not fit the gender stereotypes. We think it's fair to say that by traditional standards Tim is not very masculine and Kathy is not extremely feminine. Yet we had not been married long before we began to realize that we often saw the world very differently, and those differences couldn't all be chalked up to temperament or family or class or ethnicity. For example, Kathy was startled by Tim's ability to put his feelings and fears to one side in order to focus on the task at hand. While as a woman she of course was also more than capable of single-mindedness, Tim went about it in a very different way. Kathy saw things in Tim he would never have seen; she sees them because she's a different gender yet is close enough to notice.

As the years have gone by, we can see more ways that our marriage has made us like the two puzzle parts interlocked and forming a bigger whole. Now when things happen to Tim and he has a split second to react, he is conscious of what Kathy would think, say, or do in this situation. Tim has tangled with his wife so often that her perspective has been instilled in him. That means his repertoire of possible responses no longer includes only his own, but hers as well. In that split second he can think, *I know what Kathy would do, and is that a more wise and appropriate action than my habitual way?* And often now he does things the Kathy way.

You see, his wisdom portfolio has been permanently diversified. He's a different person, and yet he's still himself. He hasn't become more feminine. In fact, probably in many ways he's become more masculine as time has gone on. What's going on? Kathy came into Tim's life, and now he not only understands who he is better through her eyes, but he's grown. He's become who he is supposed to be only through the daily interactions, often painful, with a person who's like him, not him, opposite to him, in close.

Perhaps it does not need to be said—but we should say it anyway—that the husband is also to be a help to his wife. It's not just Eve who's brought into Adam's life with her gender resources to help him be who he's supposed to be. In Ephesians 5:25–27 it says that husbands should love their wives sacrificially as Christ loved us, and for the same purpose, to help our wives become radiant and beautiful, overcoming their faults and flaws. In a sense that's Genesis 2 in reverse. Husbands are to use their gender-differentiated resources to help their wives become who God made them to be, just as wives are to help their husbands.

But this all assumes a long journey, a drawn-out process. People do not change and become who they are meant to be overnight. We are to use our different gifts and to love each other sacrificially to help each other grow and thrive all through our lives.

It is fair to say that this is not the view of marriage that is on the rise in our culture.

Today we are consumers. Consumers are always instinctively doing cost-benefit analysis. The logic of the market, of investing and buying and selling for profit, has invaded every area of our lives, including marriage. So we look for a spouse who meets our needs, who is not high-maintenance, who won't try to change us, and who is compatible in every way. If we get into marriage with someone "like opposite" to us, who begins telling us things about ourselves we don't want to hear, we say, "This isn't right. This is supposed to be blissful. Why are we always having these confrontations?" The answer is—because you are getting *help*. And only on the far side of this discomfort will you find the person God wants you to be.

Now these first two things we need—the avoidance of idolatry, and patience for a long, sometimes difficult journey—could be seen as opposite problems. On the one hand, you have to avoid a romantic naïveté that puts your spouse on a pedestal. On the other hand, you have to avoid the anger you feel at how much work it is to love someone so different, who tells you things you don't want to hear. In Greek mythology Ulysses had to navigate his boat between the opposite sea monsters Scylla and Charybdis. If you got too close to one monster, the great danger was that you would overcorrect your course and steer into the reach and power of the other. Certainly many people have abandoned marriage idolatry only to land in the arms of deep disillusionment.

What does it take to avoid both "monsters"? How are we going to avoid expecting too much or too little from marriage?

The Joyful Humility
Only the Gospel Can Give

Genesis 2:18 says, "The LORD God said, 'It is not good for the man to be alone.'" That is a surprising statement. Why would Adam be lonely and unhappy in paradise, before there was any sin in the world? He had a perfect relationship with God; how could he be lonely? There's only one possible answer, really. God deliberately made it so that Adam would need someone besides God. That doesn't mean, of course, that our heart's *supreme* need for love isn't God. It is. What it does mean is that God designed us so that we also needed human love.

Consider what a humble, unself-centered act this is on God's part. God made human beings to need not just him, but other relationships, other selves, other hearts. The belief that God made people so he wouldn't be lonely, or so that he'd have someone to love (like having a child), or because he needed worshippers, is patently false. Yet it is nothing compared to the humility and sacrificial love God shows us later in the Bible when he says repeatedly through prophets such as Isaiah, Jeremiah, and Hosea, "I am the bridegroom, and you, my people, are the bride."

The "bridegroom" language means that solely in God do you have the lover and spouse that will satisfy you supremely. He's the ultimate "helpmeet." Martin Luther wrote about this when he said:

> A mighty fortress is our God, a bulwark never
> failing;
> Our helper He, amidst the flood of mortal ills
> prevailing

He is our help in the midst of all "mortal ills" because he is like-opposite you. He's like you because you're created in his image—you're personal and relational, as he is. But he's not like you because he's perfectly holy. You'll never become the person you're supposed to be unless he comes into your life. And to call him our "bridegroom" means he cannot be merely some entity you believe in abstractly, or even just a deity whose rules you obey. There must be intimacy in your relationship. There must be interaction. He must speak to you through his Word and you must pour out your soul to him in prayer and worship. His spousal love must be shed in your heart through the Holy Spirit (Romans 5:5). The only way you will ever avoid making an idol and savior out of your human spouse is if God is in your life as your bridegroom.

The imagery of "bridegroom" also means that in God you have the most patient and long-suffering spouse who ever existed.

The theme of God as the bridegroom of his people runs all through the Bible. In the Old Testament, of course, God calls himself the husband of Israel. But Israel constantly turned to worship other gods and in so doing she is spoken of as being guilty of spiritual adultery. Jeremiah 2–3 and Ezekiel 16 are vivid depictions of this "bad marriage," but the most famous exposition of this theme is in the book of Hosea. There God tells his prophet to marry Gomer, a woman who will be unfaithful to Hosea, "for like an adulterous wife this land [Israel] is guilty of unfaithfulness to the LORD" (Hosea 1:2).[3] And this is what happens. She goes after other lovers.

The most famous and poignant part of the story comes in the third chapter. Gomer has not only been unfaithful, she seems to have fallen into prostitution, because the only way Hosea can get her back was to purchase her from a man who owned her. God tells Hosea to do just that. Hosea writes:

> The LORD said to me, "Go, show your love to your wife again, though she is loved by another man and is an adulteress. Love her as the LORD loves the Israelites, though they turn to other gods and love the sacred raisin cakes." So I bought her for fifteen shekels of silver and about a homer and a lethek of barley. Then I told her, "You are to live with me many days; you must

not be a prostitute or be intimate with any man, and I will behave the same way toward you." (Hosea 3:1–3)

This is more than just a moving story of indefatigable love. God is hinting that, just as it requires costly self-sacrifice to love a wayward spouse, so his love for us, if it is going to be maintained, will entail cost and sacrifice on his part as well. And in Jesus's life and death we see that taken to its logical conclusion.

When the religious leaders in Matthew 9 asked Jesus, "How is it that . . . your disciples do not fast?" he replied, "How can the friends of the bridegroom mourn while he is with them?" Fasting was a religious rite that was accompanied by repentance and prayer. Jesus answered with an illustration that relied on the obvious fact that when you go to a wedding party you don't fast. (You may even go on a vacation from any diets.) But when Jesus called himself *the bridegroom* the listeners must have gasped. Everybody knew that the bridegroom of Israel was the Lord God himself—and that was who Jesus was claiming to be. Then Jesus added: "The time will come when the bridegroom will be taken from them; then they will fast" (Matthew 9:15). So he was saying two things about himself—first, that he is our divine bridegroom, and second, that he has come to die for us, to be taken away.

What the book of Hosea was hinting at we see writ large in the New Testament. God is the lover and spouse of his people. But we have given him the marriage from hell. God is in the longest-lived, worst marriage in the history of the world. We have turned to idols in our hearts, we have turned away from him, we have been absolutely terrible spouses. But God did not abandon us.

In Jesus Christ, God entered the world and paid the price to buy us away from our sin and enslavements by dying on the Cross. In essence, God says to us in the Bible: "In Jesus Christ I laid down my life for you. I did cosmically and visibly the thing that you have to do every time you try to love somebody who is flawed and imperfect. It was a substitutionary sacrifice. Your sin, your evil, your problems came onto me so that my righteousness could be put on you. Do you understand that? Now you understand how much I love you. Now you understand my delight in you." That message is the most life-changing, potent power in the world.

See how, if we rest in this reality, it gives us the greatest possible encouragement for the long journey of marriage? Remember that Jesus came to "his own" but his own received him not (John 1:11). We didn't just spurn him; we nailed him to the Cross. Some of you may be in bad marriages and may think, "Oh, my spouse is crucifying me," but in God's case it really happened. Yet Jesus loved us not because we were good, but in order to make us good. He loves us for *our* sakes, not for his sake, and so he stayed and loved us. Whenever you are ready to give up on a difficult spouse, remember Jesus's patience with you. In order to really stick with a marriage you need over and over and over again to look at your spouse and say, "You wronged me, but I wronged my great spouse, Jesus

Christ, and he kept covering me and forgiving me, so I'm loved enough by him that I can offer the same thing to you." That's the only way you'll have patience for the journey.

And, circling back, the knowledge of Christ's spousal love is also the key to the avoidance of idolatry. In Martin Luther's classic essay "On the Freedom of a Christian," he writes:

> The third incomparable grace of faith is this, that it unites the soul to Christ as the wife to a husband . . . [T]hen it follows that all they have becomes theirs in common, as well good things as evil things, so that whatsoever Christ possesses, that the believing soul may take to itself and boast of as its own, and whatever belongs to the soul, that Christ claims as his . . . Let

faith step in, and then sin, death, and hell belong to Christ, and grace, life, and salvation come to the soul. For if he is a husband, he must needs take to himself that which is his wife's, and, at the same time, impart to his wife that which is his . . . [Therefore] by the wedding ring of faith . . . the believing soul . . . becomes free from all sin, fearless of death, safe from hell, and endowed with the eternal righteousness, life, and salvation of our husband Jesus Christ.

Who can value highly enough these royal nuptials? Who can comprehend the riches of the glory of his grace? . . . From all this you will again understand why so much importance is attributed to faith, so that it alone can fulfill the law and justify without works.[4]

Luther is right that no one can "value highly enough these royal nuptials," and yet we must try. We must daily think about, savor, relish, and rejoice in Christ's spousal love to the point of growing delight. That will free us from idolizing the human love we need from our spouse; it will also give us "grace, life, and salvation" that only can be found in Jesus himself. This spouse, Jesus Christ, is the only spouse who's really going to save you. He's the only one who can really fulfill you.

Your marriage to him is the surest possible foundation for your marriage to anyone else.

The Destiny
of Marriage

Then I heard what sounded like a great multi-tude, like the roar of rushing waters and like loud peals of thunder, shouting:

> *"Hallelujah!*
> *For our Lord God Almighty reigns.*
> *Let us rejoice and be glad*
> *and give him glory!*
> *For the wedding of the Lamb has come,*
> *and his bride has made herself ready.*
> *Fine linen, bright and clean,*
> *was given her to wear."*

—REVELATION 19:6–8

Then I saw "a new heaven and a new earth," for the first heaven and the first earth had passed away, and there was no longer any sea. I saw the

Holy City, the new Jerusalem, coming down out of heaven from God, prepared as a bride beautifully dressed for her husband.

—REVELATION 21:1-2

Marriage is a journey that traditionally has been said to have an ending— "till death do us part." In one sense death certainly does end a marriage. The surviving spouse is free to marry again, for example. Yet the Christian understanding is that marriage prepares us for an eternal union of which our earthly marriage was only a foretaste. And even the relationship two Christians have in marriage here in this world need not be seen as something that is ended or even diminished by death.

To understand the true destiny of marriage, we need to look at sex, at the goal of history, and at the resurrection itself.

The Signpost of Sex

Many people have pointed out that the Bible is not a prudish book. It is often celebratory about the beauty and pleasures of sexual love, as seen in the verses in Proverbs 5:18–20 that tell a husband to be ravished with his wife's breasts, or the entire book of the Song of Solomon. But the Bible goes beyond frankness, and even fun, when it talks about sex. It goes to glory.

In Romans 7 the apostle Paul likens Christians to a woman who has been married "to the law." That is, we have been trying to save ourselves by our performance—whether that means religious observance of God's moral law or the pursuit of wealth, career, or some cause. But when we believe in Christ we become married "to him who was raised from the dead, that we might bear fruit to God" (Romans 7:4). This is a daring image. As a wife puts herself into the arms of her husband, and children are born into the world through her body, so we put ourselves in the arms of Jesus and then we also bear fruit—of our own changed lives (Galatians 5:22–23) or of good works that change the lives of others (Colossians 1:6, 10).[1]

Some commentators have struggled with Paul's imagery here, calling it "undignified," and indeed it is somewhat breathtaking.[2] But the metaphor seems clear enough. In some sense married sexuality, which can create new life, points to the ultimate love relationship with Jesus Christ. Union with him by faith gives us the supreme experience of love, which can in turn bear transformative, life-generating fruit. That relationship, as Paul says, begins now, and so can the fruit bearing. But the Bible tells us elsewhere that the communion with Christ and his love that we have now is only a very dim hint of what it will be like to see him face-to-face (1 Corinthians 13:12).

The Bible tells us that we currently know our Spouse only by faith, not by sight (2 Corinthians 5:7). The love we experience here can only ever be partial. But when we actually see him face-to-face, the transformation of his love and the fulfillment of our being will be complete (1 John 3:2–3).

What do all these passages about Jesus being our husband and bridegroom mean? It means at least this—that sex in marriage is both a pointer to and a foretaste of the joy of that perfect future world of love. In heaven when we know him directly, we enter into a union of love with him and all other people who love him. On that great day there's going to be deep delight, towering joy, and deep security of which the most rapturous sex between a man and a woman is just an echo.

As we saw before, 1 Corinthians 6 tells us that sex outside of marriage is wrong. But in this text Saint Paul does not merely give a bare prohibition—he explains *why* it is wrong for a Christian.

> Whoever is united with the Lord is one with him in spirit. Flee from sexual immorality . . . Whoever sins sexually sins against their own body. Do you not know that your bodies are temples of the Holy Spirit, who is in you, whom you have received from

God? You are not your own. (1 Corinthians 6:17–19)

Paul reminds us (as in Romans 7:4) that we are married to Christ, and so the Holy Spirit comes to dwell in us. Therefore, he reasons, we must not do anything sexually with our bodies that does not reflect and mirror that relationship to him. When we unite with Christ we give ourselves wholly and exclusively and permanently to him, as he sacrificed himself for us. In the same way we must never have sex apart from giving our whole lives, exclusively and permanently, to a spouse. Any other use of sex fails to let it be what God made it to be: a signpost of our union with him, present and future.

That's what the Bible teaches about sex, and that goes far beyond just "sex positivity."

Many people today were raised being told that "sex is dangerous and kind of dirty." Then people started to overcorrect for that by saying, "Sex is a good thing that brings pleasure and fulfillment, and you can use it anyway you want as long as it's consensual."

The Bible's vision for sex is infinitely higher than either of these views, and it is not anything in the middle. Sex is not dirty—it was made by God and he pronounced it "good" (Genesis 1:26–31). But sex is far more than just an appetite such as eating.

The glory of God in the face of Jesus is the beauty and love we have been looking for all our lives. "In your face is fullness of joy; in your right hand are pleasures forevermore" (Psalm 16:13). We will finally know the fulfillment of our natures, the infinite satisfaction of his presence (Psalm 17:15).

Will that day be pleasurable? Of course. And that's why sex, its earthly analogy, is fun and pleasurable. But sex can be far more than a momentary thrill if we align it in time and space with what it points to in the future. We must use it as a way to say to someone else: "I belong completely, exclusively, and permanently to you." When we do that, it becomes not a way to get pleasure from someone, but a deeply unitive act, a way to cement two human lives into a single entity and community, and a way to shape your heart so as to love sacrificially as Jesus loved us. Only in the context of marriage does sex reach its complete potential to delight and fulfill.

So sex, like marriage itself, points to something beyond itself. If we don't see that and set our hearts on that future, sex and marriage will always bitterly disappoint us.

The End of History

As Luther says, in keeping with Saint Paul's views, we are in one sense already married to Christ. But there is another sense in which we are not yet married—we are more like engaged to him. Revelation tells us "the marriage supper of the lamb" is a future day in which we will be married to Jesus (Revelation 19:7). The great wedding day in which we fall into his arms is the only wedding day that will really make everything right in our lives.

It is significant that the Bible begins in Genesis with a wedding, and that wedding's original purpose was to fill the world with children of God. But Adam and Eve turned from God and the first wedding failed to fulfill its purpose.

When we come to the end of the Bible we

see the church "coming down out of heaven from God, prepared as a bride beautifully dressed for her husband." The echoes of Genesis 2 are unmistakable. Again we see God bringing a bride to her husband, only this time the husband is Jesus and we are the bride. In that first marriage Adam failed to step in and help his wife when she needed him. But at the end of time there will be another wedding, the marriage supper of the Lamb, and *its* purpose is also to fill the world with children of God. *It* will succeed where the first marriage failed because, while the first husband in history failed, the Second Husband does not. The true Adam, Jesus Christ, will never fail his spouse, the Second Eve, his church.

Let's also notice something new that was not mentioned in Genesis. It says that we, his people, will be dressed beautifully for our husband. Of course the primary reason there is no mention of a wedding dress in the Garden of Eden is that Adam and Eve were "naked and unashamed." That was, however, before the coming of sin. The Bible often talks metaphorically about our need to have our sin covered by clean or beautiful garments (Psalm 32; Ezekiel 16; Zechariah 3). If we are to be beautiful to our husband, we will have to have our sins covered by his grace and righteousness (Philippians 3:9). And the image of the wedding dress conveys this in a wonderful way.

Wedding garments are designed to make us feel beautiful—like our best possible selves. These clothes are a great metaphor for how Jesus covers our sins and clothes us in his righteousness, at infinite cost to himself. The gospel is that Christ lived the beautiful and good life that we should live but have not. But now, by faith, his beauty rests upon us. When we believe, we get his righteousness, as Martin Luther explained. Revelation tells us that we, in a sense, will come down the aisle to Jesus and we will look beautiful to him. Can you grasp how astonishing that is?

As a minister I have had the privilege of standing beside the groom in hundreds of weddings. My wife and I always watch the groom in the moment before the arrival of the bride. You can tell *exactly* when he catches sight of her as she comes through a doorway or turns a corner and suddenly—there she is. The groom catches his breath and his heart leaps when he sees her looking so radiant. The radiance on his face echoes hers as they gaze on each other.

Is the Bible really saying that Jesus finds us beautiful like that? That we will have that kind of love from the Lord of the universe? Yes. This is what it means to be "in Christ," what it means to belong to him. Of course we can only partially comprehend this intellectually and experientially. 1 John 3:2 says: "Dear friends . . . what we will be has not yet been made known. But we know that when Christ appears we shall be like him, for we shall see him as he is." The first sight of his beauty and glory, and the first direct experience of his love, will immediately transform us into spotless persons of "freedom and glory" (Romans 8:21). That's in the future, of course, but then John adds: "All who have this hope in him purify themselves just as he is pure" (3:3). This future beatific vision and wedding supper will be so powerful, John says, that to even hope for it—to get the barest foretaste of it and to rest in our assurance of it—begins to transform us now.

As we rejoice in the spousal love of Jesus we will be changed. Fears, jealousies, resentments, boredom, disillusionments, loneliness—all the things that darken our lives—will diminish. And only if you look beyond the end of your earthly marriage to your union with Christ will you love your husband or wife well.

You must shed the illusion of thinking, "If I can just find *the one* and get married, then my life will be OK." No. There is only one "the One," and he awaits you at the end of time, at the feast. When you see his glory it will make up for a million terrible lifetimes.

And the beauty he will put on you that day will outshine the best wedding dress you've ever seen.

The End of Marriage?

In Matthew 22 we read of the Sadducees, a party of leaders in ancient Israel who did not believe in a future resurrection of the dead. They knew Jesus believed and taught it and so they tried to trap him. They presented a hypothetical case. There were seven brothers and the first one married a wife. He died, however, and she married the second brother. Then he died, and she married the next brother. On this went until she had married all seven men and they all died. "Now then," they concluded, "at the resurrection, whose wife will she be of the seven, since all of them were married to her?"

Jesus began his answer by saying, "You are in error because you do not know the Scriptures or the power of God" (Matthew 22:29). Not only did they not know the Bible, but their God was too small. They had no true sense of his infinite wisdom, glory, and love. They couldn't really imagine him creating much of a different world than the one we have now.

As for the teaching of the Bible, Jesus says:

> "Have you not read what God said to you, 'I am the God of Abraham, the God of Isaac, and the God of Jacob'? He is not the God of the dead but of the living." (Matthew 22:31–32)

God never says, "I *was* the God of Abraham, Isaac, and Jacob." Though it was centuries after their deaths when he spoke these words to Moses (Exodus 3:6), God never speaks about them as if his relationship with them was in the past tense. "I *am* their God," the Lord says, and Jesus adds, "God is not the God of the dead but of the living." In other words, no one who has the true God as their God is ever really dead. One biblical scholar explained Jesus's saying this way: "Those with whom the living God identifies himself cannot be truly dead, and therefore they must be alive with him after their earthly life is finished."[3] In this Jesus establishes the general principle that to unite with God through faith is to be destined for a greater life beyond the end of this one.

Then Jesus says, speaking directly to the

Sadducees' hypothetical case: "At the resurrection people will neither marry nor be given in marriage; they will be like the angels in heaven" (Matthew 22:30).

At first, this seems to mean that death is, indeed, the end of our marriages. Certainly, in the resurrection we will be "like the angels" in that there will be no need for procreation in order to replenish the population. There will be no death, and so we can imagine why an institution that was largely dedicated to the birth and nurture of new life would not be necessary.

But R. T. France, in his commentary on Matthew, poses a question that hangs in the air as we hear Jesus's words. He writes: "Those who have found some of the deepest joys of earthly life in the special bond of a married relationship may be dismayed to hear that

that must be left behind." However, France notices that Jesus's terms "marry" and "giving in marriage" are two verbs that refer to the custom of the bride's father giving a bride away and to the act of the bridegroom in receiving her. In other words, Jesus is saying that the active pairing off into marriage will not continue. Then France adds:

> But note that what Jesus declares to be inappropriate in heaven is marriage, not love. [Why couldn't it be that] heavenly relationships are not something *less* than marriage, but something *more*[?] He does not say that the love between those who have been married on earth will vanish, but rather implies that it will be broadened so that no one is excluded."[4]

C. S. Lewis in *The Four Loves* speaks of a close trio of friends—Jack (C. S. Lewis), Ronald (J. R. R. Tolkien), and Charles (Charles Williams). When Charles died, Lewis noticed that he did not as a consequence get "more" of Ronald. The things in Ronald that only Charles could draw out were now lost to Jack. In other words, the more he shared Ronald's friendship with others, the more of it he had himself. Lewis concluded that this was a faint image of the perfect love relationships we will have in heaven, when jealousy and selfishness will be gone.[5]

So in the question posed by the Sadducees, which of the brothers will the woman be married to in the resurrection? The answer is— she will be wife to all of them and then some. (This is a good answer to hear if you have had a spouse die and have subsequently had another good marriage.) The answer is everyone will be in the closest possible love relationship with everyone else, because Christ's perfect love will be flowing in and out of us like a fountain, like a river.

Will we still be with our earthly spouse in heaven, in the resurrection? Certainly. Look at Jesus, the first born from the dead. When he encountered people he knew, as on the road to Emmaus in Luke 24, he had been changed enough that they did not know him at first, and yet then they recognized him. He was still himself, though now with a perfect, resurrected body. His friends were still his friends.

And who better than your spouse of many years will be able to rejoice in your new resurrected self? When all your sins and flaws are removed from your soul and body your spouse will be able to say with infinite joy, "I always knew you could be like this. I saw it in you. But now look at you!"

In the letter by John Newton to newly-weds cited earlier, he writes about the relationship we will have with each other beyond death:

> So sure as you are joined you must part, and such separations are hard to flesh and blood; but it will only be a separation for a little time. You will walk together as fellow-heirs of eternal life, helpmeets and partakers of each other's spiritual joys, and at length you shall meet before the throne of glory, and be for ever with the Lord. May you live under the influence of these views, and find every sweet made still

sweeter by the shining of the Sun of Righteousness upon your souls; and every cross sanctified to lead you to a nearer, more immediate, and more absolute dependence on himself.[6]

The end of your earthly marriage will be nothing less than an entrance into an endless feast, where you will be joined to your earthly partner in ways you could never realize in this world, as well as with all others and with Jesus, "Lover of your soul."

Acknowledgments

For this book and the series of which it is a part, we owe even more thanks than usual to our editor at Viking, Brian Tart. It was Brian who saw the short meditation on death that Tim preached at the funeral of Terry Hall, Kathy's sister. He proposed that we turn it not only into one but three short books on birth, marriage, and death. We also thank our many friends in South Carolina who made it possible to write this and the companion books while at Folly Beach last summer.

Notes

Beginning a Marriage

1. From "The Order for the Solemnization of Marriage" in the Presbyterian *Book of Common Worship* (Philadelphia: Presbyterian Board of Publication, 1906), and Genesis 2:22–24.

2. Belinda Luscombe, "Why 25% of Millennials Will Never Get Married," *Time*, September 24, 2014, time.com/3422624 /report-millennials-marriage/.

3. See Robert Bellah et al., *Habits of the Heart: Individualism and Commitment in American Life* (Berkeley and Los Angeles, CA: University of California Press, 2007).

4. "Where You Are," lyrics by Mark Mancina and Lin-Manuel Miranda, from *Moana* (2016). This is ironically a very Western, individualistic approach to identity being awkwardly superimposed on a (fictional) girl in a non-Western culture. That is

certainly within the scope of artistic license, but it's fair to point out that it is an example of how contemporary Western secular people think of their worldview as a universal truth that can improve the cultures of the rest of the world.

5. Jennifer B. Rhodes, cited in Marissa Hermanson, "How Millennials Are Redefining Marriage," Gottman Institute, *Gottman Relationship Blog*, July 3, 2018, www.gottman.com/blog/millennials-redefining-marriage/.

6. Just one sample of many studies: W. Bradford Wilcox, "The New Progressive Argument: For Kids, Marriage Per Se Doesn't Matter," Institute for Family Studies, September 15, 2014, ifstudies.org/blog/for-kids-marriage-per-se-doesnt-matter-right/.

7. Wendell Berry, "Sex, Economy, Freedom, and Community," *Sex, Economy, Freedom, and Community* (New York: Pantheon, 1993), 119.

8. Joe Pinsker, "How Successful Are the Marriages of People with Divorced Parents?" *Atlantic*, May 30, 2019.

9. Pinsker, "How Successful Are the Marriages of People with Divorced Parents?" I added the italics in the quotation.

10. Linda J. Waite et al., "Does Divorce Make People Happy? Findings from a Study of Unhappy Marriages," Institute for American Values, 2002, http://www.americanvalues.org/search/item.php?id=13.

11. Pinsker, "How Successful Are the Marriages of People with Divorced Parents?"

12. Paula England, "Is the Retreat from Marriage Due to Cheap Sex, Men's Waning Job Prospects, or Both?" Institute for Family Studies, November 1, 2017, ifstudies.org/blog/is-the-retreat-from-marriage-due-to-cheap-sex-mens-waning-job-prospects-or-both.

13. Kyle Harper, *From Shame to Sin: The Christian Transformation of Sexual Morality in Late Antiquity* (Cambridge, MA: Harvard University Press, 2016), 86. Also see all of Harper's chapter 2, "The Will and the World in Early Christian Sexuality," 80–133.

14. Courtney Sender, "He Asked Permission to Touch, but Not to Ghost," *New York Times*, September 7, 2018.

15. Sender, "He Asked Permission to Touch, but Not to Ghost."

16. Sender, "He Asked Permission to Touch, but Not to Ghost."

17. Quoted in Carolyn Kaufman, "Why Finding a Life Partner Isn't That Simple," *Psychology Today*, April 20, 2013.

18. Caveat: If you have been living together before marriage (and I hope you have not, as that is not a good preparation for marriage), these suggestions still apply to you. See Timothy and Kathy Keller, *The Meaning of Marriage* (New York: Penguin, 2011) Introduction. Living together is very different from actually being married. The knowledge that "the back door is always unlocked" and can be used if anything goes really sour means that you don't have to stick around for the hard work of relationship building, problem solving, and family nurturing.

19. Judson Swihart, *How Do You Say "I Love You"?* (Downers Grove, IL: InterVarsity Press, 1977). A much more well-known and recent popular book on this subject is Gary Chapman's *The 5 Love Languages: The Secret to Love That Lasts* (Chicago: Northfield Publishing, 2010).

20. Swihart, *How Do You Say "I Love You"?*, 15.

Notes

Sustaining a Marriage

1. John Newton and Richard Cecil, *The Works of John Newton*, vol. 6 (London: Hamilton, Adams & Co., 1824), 132–33.
2. C. S. Lewis, *The Four Loves* (New York: HarperCollins, 2017), 157.
3. For a major study of the theme of "God as our spouse," see Raymond C. Ortlund Jr., *God's Unfaithful Wife: A Biblical Theology of Spiritual Adultery* (Downers Grove, IL: IVP Academic, 2003).
4. Text from *First Principles of the Reformation*, ed. by Henry Wace and C. A. Buchheim (London: John Murray, 1883), can be found at https://sourcebooks.fordham.edu/mod/luther-freedomchristian.asp.

The Destiny of Marriage

1. "The Fruitful Bride" in Francis Schaeffer, *True Spirituality* (Wheaton, IL: Tyndale House, 2001), 72–81.
2. See the discussion by John Murray, *The*

Epistle to the Romans, single-volume edition (Grand Rapids, MI: William B. Eerdmans, 1971), 244, and especially n7.

3. R. T. France, *The Gospel of Matthew*, The New International Commentary on the New Testament (Grand Rapids, MI: William B. Eerdmans, 2007), 840–41.

4. France, *The Gospel of Matthew*, 839.

5. C. S. Lewis, *The Four Loves* (New York: HarperCollins, 2017), 78–79.

6. John Newton and Richard Cecil, *The Works of John Newton*, vol. 6 (London: Hamilton, Adams & Co., 1824), 132–33.

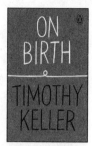

ON BIRTH

If life is a journey, there are few events as significant as birth, marriage, and death. In *On Birth*, bestselling author Timothy Keller explains the deeper Christian understanding of birth and baptism.

ON DEATH

In a culture that largely avoids thinking about the inevitability of death, Timothy Keller celebrates the Christian resources of hope in the face of death. Slim and compelling, *On Death* gives us the tools to understand God's triumph over death through the work of Jesus.

PENGUIN BOOKS

ON BIRTH

Timothy Keller started Redeemer Presbyterian Church in New York City with his wife, Kathy, and their three sons. Redeemer grew to nearly 5,500 regular Sunday attendees and helped to start more than three hundred new churches around the world. In 2017 Keller moved from his role as senior minister at Redeemer to the staff of Redeemer City to City, an organization that helps national church leaders around the world reach and minister in global cities. He is the author of *The Prodigal Prophet*, *God's Wisdom for Navigating Life*, as well as *The Meaning of Marriage*, *The Prodigal God*, and *The Reason for God*, among others.

ALSO BY TIMOTHY KELLER

The Reason for God
The Prodigal God
Counterfeit Gods
Generous Justice
Jesus the King
Center Church
Every Good Endeavor
Walking with God Through Pain and Suffering
Encounters with Jesus
Prayer
Preaching
Making Sense of God
Hidden Christmas
The Prodigal Prophet
On Death

WITH KATHY KELLER
The Meaning of Marriage
The Songs of Jesus
God's Wisdom for Navigating Life
The Meaning of Marriage: A Couple's Devotional
On Marriage

On Birth

TIMOTHY
KELLER

PENGUIN BOOKS

PENGUIN BOOKS
An imprint of Penguin Random House LLC
penguinrandomhouse.com

All Bible references are from the New International Version
(NIV), unless otherwise noted.

ISBN 9780143135357 (paperback)
ISBN 9780525507017 (ebook)

Printed in the United States of America
1   3   5   7   9   10   8   6   4   2

Set in Adobe Garamond · Designed by Sabrina Bowers

To our grandchildren;
the joy we felt at your births
could only be exceeded by the knowledge
that you have experienced the new birth.

Contents

Introduction to the
How to Find God Series · *xi*

First Birth · *1*

Second Birth · *41*

Growing in Grace · *85*

Acknowledgments · *115*

Notes · *117*

Introduction to the How to Find God Series

L ife is a journey, and finding and knowing God is fundamental to that journey. When a new child is born, when we approach marriage, and when we find ourselves facing death—either in old age or much earlier—it tends to concentrate the mind. We shake ourselves temporarily free from absorption in the whirl of daily life and ask the big questions of the ages:

Am I living for things that matter?

Will I have what it takes to face this new stage of life?

Do I have a real relationship with God?

The most fundamental transition any human being can make is what the Bible refers to as the new birth (John 3:1–8), or becoming a "new creation" (2 Corinthians 5:17). This can happen at any time in a life, of course, but often the circumstances that lead us to vital faith in Christ occur during these tectonic shifts in life stages. Over forty-five years of ministry, my wife, Kathy, and I have seen that people are particularly open to exploring a relationship with God at times of major life transition.

In this series of short books we want to help readers facing major life changes to think about

what constitutes the truly changed life. Our purpose is to give readers the Christian foundations for life's most important and profound moments. We start with birth and baptism, move into marriage, and conclude with death. My hope is that these slim books will provide guidance, comfort, wisdom, and, above all, will help point the way to finding and knowing God all throughout your life.

On Birth

First Birth

Born to raise us from the earth;
Born to give us second birth.

—"HARK! THE HERALD ANGELS SING,"

CHARLES WESLEY

he Christian faith teaches that every person should experience two births. In one's first birth you are born into the natural world. Then, in what Charles Wesley calls our "second birth," which Jesus himself describes as being "born again" (John 3:3), we are born into the kingdom of God and receive new spiritual life. The first birth is ours because God is our Creator; the second birth can be ours because God is also our Redeemer. The Lord is the author of both.

In light of this, we want to consider the spiritual issues surrounding both births. What does it mean to receive a new human life from God? What are the responsibilities of the family and the church to newborns? How can we help our children who are with us through the first birth come to experience the second birth?

Fearful and Wonderful

Rather than directly creating each new human being himself, the Lord bestowed on the union of male and female the unique power to bring new human beings into the world. No wonder

2

then that newborn babies in the Bible are always regarded with wonder as signs of God's blessing. The original charge of God to the human
race was: "Be fruitful, and multiply and fill the
earth" (Genesis 1:28). While God does not demand that all people be married, as Jesus himself and Saint Paul demonstrate, nevertheless,
Genesis 1:28 explains why we feel so deeply that
we are witnessing a miracle of God when gazing
on a newborn child. Psalm 127:3 says that *all*
children are a "reward" from God.

But there is another side to it.

God often sends heroes and deliverers into the
world by giving them as newborns to couples
who are disconsolate because they cannot have
children. So Isaac, Jacob, Joseph, Samson, and
Samuel are all born to women who previously
could not conceive. And yet a quick survey of
their lives, particularly those of Jacob, Joseph,

and Samson, reveals that these children, who were direct "gifts of God," were also great heart-griefs to their parents.

Something of this is seen in this famous passage in Psalm 139:13–16: "For you created my inmost being; you knit me together in my mother's womb. I praise you because I am *fearfully and wonderfully* made . . . Your eyes saw my unformed body; all the days ordained for me were written in your book." As one Bible scholar put it: "Our pre-natal fashioning by God [is] a powerful reminder of the value He sets on us, even as embryos, and of His planning our end from the beginning."[1]

The phrase we are "fearfully and wonderfully made" is full of interest. Every baby born into the world is a wonderful creation, but at the same time a frightening one. Anyone who looks on a newborn—realizing this is a new human life in the image of the Creator, come into the world along with particular gifts and callings and a life planned by the Lord of history—must respond with a kind of fear and trembling. And no one should behold a child with more awe and fear than the child's parents.

When Kathy and I brought home our first-born, I was surprised to see her cuddle him close and weep. Partly this was her hormones talking, she said, but partly it was a recognition of what we had let this tiny little person in for as a member of a fallen race. Yes, "all the days ordained for him" were "written in God's book," but as an adult she knew that our son's book would contain disappointment, hurt, failure, pain, loss, and ultimately his own death. All this would happen no matter how hard we would try to shield him. So she literally trembled before the responsibility of being a parent to this wonder of the universe. And when I thought about it, so did I.

Kathy concluded:

> The birth of a child has been referred to by one mother as a "family-quake." Whether it is joyful and desired or not, the first or fourteenth, healthy or challenged, a new person entering the world alters history in ways both large and small just by reason of his or her existence. As a new parent, you have entered a fellowship stretching back millennia, one that includes queens and slaves, thirteen-year-olds in ancient cultures and at least one ninety-year-old mother, Sarah, mother of Isaac, in the Bible. Every

kingdom, tribe, tongue, and nation has its rituals surrounding giving birth, and for a reason. It is a near-mystical event, welcoming a person who was not-there but now *is*.

Blessing or Burden?

Bringing new life into the world is the most tremendous, astonishing thing a human being can do. Women are especially given the privilege of receiving and nurturing new life, being subcreators with God. In willingly receiving the embrace of the masculine, the power granted to the female sex is unleashed, and new, formerly nonexistent life blooms into the world.[2] Not only does the creation of new life propel civilization and culture into the next generation in its myriad forms; it also changes those of us in the current generation in countless ways, demanding sacrifice on a scale you may never before have attempted.

But modern people are ambivalent about this immense privilege, to say the least.

The fear (if not the wonder) of children is something modern people see very clearly. We live in a society that has seen a sharp decline in the birth rate, to the point that there are not enough births to replace deaths—the so-called replacement rate. Fewer people today see children as a blessing.

Liberals tend to blame economic factors and conservatives tend to point to the rising tide of selfishness. One of the better books about this is *All Joy and No Fun: The Paradox of Modern Parenthood* by Jennifer Senior, because the author is careful not to overgeneralize. She lists numerous reasons for the contemporary ambivalence toward parenting, but two stand out.

The first is the unprecedented emphasis in modern culture on personal autonomy and self-realization. We have more freedom to choose our careers, our sexual practices, our geographical location, whether to marry and stay married, whether to have children or not. "Few of us would want to reverse the historical advance that gave us our newfound freedoms," she writes, but we have "come to define liberty negatively, as lack of dependence, the right not to be obligated to others . . . [and] to mean immunity from social claims on one's wealth or time."[3]

Because we strongly conceive of liberty as freedom from obligation, "parenthood is a dizzying shock." We have now been given the right to choose or change anything that does not seem to be satisfying or benefiting us—job, location, career, spouse. "But we can never choose or change our children. They are the last binding obligation in a culture that asks for almost no other permanent commitments at all."[4]

I don't think the "dizzying shock" to parents can simply be read as rank selfishness. Rather, parenting challenges all the habits of the heart that our culture has formed in us around relationships. Changing those habits is neither easy nor simple.

The other reason that modern parenthood is so paradoxical is that parents pour more emotional and financial capital into raising their children than ever, so much so that parenting "may have become . . . its own profession, so to speak." There is only one problem with this job: "its goals are far from clear." What are parents trying to actually *do* with their children? For example, "today's parents are . . . charged with the psychological well-being of their sons and daughters, which on the face of it is a laudable goal. But it's a murky one."[5] Indeed—who defines "psychological well-being"? Does it simply mean happiness? Can't cruel people be happy? Then is the goal to make them moral and good? Even though contemporary parents may want that, they live in a culture that insists moral values are culturally constructed. And usually people throw in that we should not impose our values on our children but let them choose their own. Really? Should we not care if they are not becoming honest, compassionate, fair dealing, and patient? Are those things we can let them choose—or not?

Christians have resources that speak directly to these challenges. To begin with, the biblical teaching about human nature reframes parental expectations. Modern child psychology

11

literature—and more popular, informal folk wisdom about parenting—always, inevitably, assumes some philosophical anthropology, some view of human nature that underlies everything else. It may be positive about our ability to shape our lives through our own choices or pessimistic about it. It may see human nature as basically good or as irremediably bad. The Bible, however, tells us that human beings are far greater *and* worse than we can imagine. We are made in God's image but deeply marred by our own sin. As C. S. Lewis's main character says to the human children in his *Chronicles of Narnia*:

> "You come of the Lord Adam and the Lady Eve," said Aslan. "And that is both honor enough to erect the head of the poorest beggar, and shame enough to

bow the shoulders of the greatest em-
peror on earth. Be content."[6]

This Christian view of human nature helps parents learn from—without fully accepting—a
host of more reductionistic approaches to child
development. There is more "conservative" literature that stresses things like discipline, limits,
and the teaching of moral values, as well as
more "progressive" materials that emphasize listening to children, strong affirmation, and giving them freedom to question and think for
themselves. The Christian view of human beings as fallen bearers of the divine image can
borrow from and learn from all of them without embracing their more simplistic views of the
human heart.

Beyond this critical understanding of human

nature, Christianity gives us other resources that directly address the challenges that parents have always felt and feel today.

Giving Your Child

Children are a joy, but parents often sense a responsibility that can be overwhelming. The Christian church offers, in response, the sacrament of baptism.[7] While not all Christians practice infant baptism, most have some way of publicly dedicating their children to God, which follows the Jewish practice. After Jesus's birth we are told: "Joseph and Mary took him to Jerusalem to present him to the Lord" (Luke 2:22).

When we bring our children to God in baptism, it does not confer salvation automatically on the child. Just as God does not magically create new human beings but does it through the union of a man and a woman, so he normally brings about our second birth much like our first birth—through love relationships and, so often, through the family.

Sin tends to run in families. We see weaknesses in our parents and grandparents that show up in us even though we dislike the traits, even when we try with all our might to avoid them. But *grace* tends to run in families, too. Love and good models of faith and grace can lead a child to seek those things for himself or herself.

Baptizing your child is an enormous help to parents. It is a public service with vows, surrounded by friends in the Christian church community. Modern people have virtually abandoned public promises (except for weddings)—and they therefore have neglected a powerful mechanism for shaping character. To make solemn promises before the faces of family and friends molds us and makes permanent impressions on our minds, hearts, and wills.

In baptism parents take binding, covenantal oaths. We promise to grow in grace ourselves (see "Growing in Grace") in order to attract our children not so much to us but to our Savior and Lord. We promise to bring the child up not in isolation but in the midst of a church community that is united by promises to God and one another. Ordinarily those surrounding us at baptism make verbal public vows to support us and care for our children as well. Our community rallies around us and we feel reinforced for the calling and mission of parenthood. And while baptism may not save the child, we believe real divine grace and strength from God comes down in response to these vows, as our God is a covenant God who honors promises (Psalm 56:12–13).

There are almost as many sets of baptismal parental promises as there are denominations, but one set always has stood out to us:

To the Parents

1. Do you acknowledge that you are saved only through faith in Jesus, not through anything you have done or ever will do, but only through His finished work—His death upon the Cross—by which He took upon Himself the penalty for your sins?

2. Do you realize that baptism is not a saving ordinance, and though it signifies your child's membership in the covenant community, it is not a matter of magic? Do you understand that your child is responsible to receive Christ as Savior and Lord as she [or he] becomes accountable to Him?

3. Have you covenanted with God to give back this child to Him, so that, if He sees fit in His providence to call this child home to Himself, you will not complain against Him, or if she [or he] grows to adulthood and is called to serve God in a faraway place, you will not stand in her [or his] way but rather encourage her [or him]?

4. Do you in this sacrament covenant together with God to raise your child in the instruc-

tion, obedience, and worship of the Lord, to pray for and with her [or him], to keep her [or him] in the fellowship of God's people, to be faithful and loving in your home, to be godly examples of faith yourselves, and therefore to do your utmost to lead her [or him] to a saving knowledge of Christ?

To the Congregation

Do you, the members of this congregation, agree to pray for these parents as they raise their children in the Christian faith, and to support them in their efforts by providing their children with further examples of obedience and service to God? Should these parents neglect their God-given task, will you in all humility rebuke and correct them?[8]

Raising Your Child

Dedicating your child to God through public promises before the congregation directs parents to a number of practices that are designed to turn a child's heart toward God. Western secular culture presents many unique challenges to Christian parents who want to do this.

Our society's cultural institutions hold many faith assumptions about human nature and morality, yet secular people generally do not recognize them as beliefs at all. We absorb the reigning narratives of the culture through commercials, movies and TV episodes, social media, and innumerable other forms—"You have to be true to yourself"; "You have to do what makes you happy and not sacrifice it"; "You should be free to live as you choose as long as you harm no one else"; "No one has the right to tell anyone else what is right or wrong for them"; "You have to live your own truth." Each of these statements is at sharp variance with biblical teaching on discipleship, on sin and grace, and on the character of God. Every one of them assumes highly debatable beliefs about human purpose and identity, yet they are presented as beyond question—as being simply objective, reasonable, open-minded, and scientific. Social theorists call this "mystification"—creating the impression that contestable arguments are really unassailable facts about reality.

A good example of this can be seen in a *New York Times Magazine* article about sex. The writer says that for centuries traditional societies "condemned as aberrant sexual pleasures we now know are healthy."[9] But those older cultures did not think that the sexual practices were "unhealthy"—rather, that they were wrong.

They were making moral judgments. The writer, however, does not say that "now we know that there are no moral norms regarding sex"—even though that is what she means. Instead the author cloaks her beliefs about sex, which are in many ways a throwback to the beliefs of ancient Greco-Roman culture, in the language of science.

Parents who want to see their child's heart turn toward Christ and his gospel must come to grips with the ways that the culture mystifies its beliefs as commonsense truths. Young people daily spend hours on social media, where immersive waves of stories, testimonies, movies, videos, commercials, and music convey a worldview of secular modernity.

If you think that merely taking a child to church or sending them to a youth group once a week will be sufficient to overcome all this and form them as thoughtful Christians, you are wrong. What will most likely happen is that inwardly their deepest habits of the heart and instinctive ways of judgment will become disconnected from the Bible stories they still publicly profess. At some point in their late teens or college years, Christianity will begin to seem implausible.

What can parents do? James D. Hunter is a sociologist who has studied "character formation" curricula used in schools across the United States. Each curriculum seeks to produce honesty, justice, kindness, generosity, wisdom, self-control, and other virtues in students. However, Hunter shows that all the various courses and materials, whether used in public or private schools, secular or religious schools, show no evidence that they actually produce character change in pupils.[10]

Martin Luther King, Jr., is regularly lifted up by these curricula as a model of the virtue of justice, and students are exhorted to emulate him. But, Hunter asks, how did Martin Luther King, Jr., become the man he became? He was the product of a rich and strong community, the African-American church, which gave its people not just ethical principles, but a "cosmology." This is a way to understand the universe through the story of the God of the book of Exodus, the God who liberates. This story was not taught by the church as simply an inspirational account of something that happened in the past, but rather as a story that explains all of history and in which people can live today.

In short, what produced a Martin Luther

King, Jr., was a robust community that actually incarnated and lived out a clear moral vision, based on a set of beliefs about where the world came from, who human beings are, and where they are going.[11] Obviously classrooms cannot produce all this, but families can, especially if they are embedded in a particular church community.

Hunter calls this a moral ecology. It consists of mutually reinforcing communities in which the children live, such as church and home (and sometimes also school), where a particular vision and story of the world, and of the moral values that flow from it, are taught, explained, embodied, and applied to daily life. The features of such a shaping community always include a moral cosmology and sourcebook, as well as moral discourse, imagination, and modeling.

A Moral Ecology

In Deuteronomy 6 the Bible gives us a glimpse of
the moral ecology that Christian parents must inhabit with their children if they are to be formed
as thoughtful Christians with gospel-based moral
character. The beginning of the chapter provides
the goal of character formation.

> These are the commands, decrees and
> laws the LORD your God directed me to
> teach you to observe in the land that
> you are crossing the Jordan to possess,
> so that you, your children and their
> children after them may fear the LORD
> your God as long as you live by keeping
> all his decrees and commands that I
> give you, and so that you may enjoy
> long life. Hear, Israel, and be careful to

> obey so that it may go well with you
> and that you may increase greatly in a
> land flowing with milk and honey, just
> as the LORD, the God of your ancestors,
> promised you. (Deuteronomy 6:1–3)

The goal is not just ethical behavior ("keep all his decrees and commands") but also an inner awe and wonder toward the greatness of God ("the fear of the Lord"). This is a changed heart, not mere behavioral compliance. What is needed are habits of the heart in which we find God the greatest source of our meaning, identity, hope, and happiness. How can such a heart be nurtured?

Moral principles only make sense if they are grounded in a *moral cosmology*—a picture of a universe that supports them. Here we see that if we obey his commandments "it [will] go well with you" and "you may enjoy long life" (verse 3). The God of the Bible is our loving Creator, who has designed us for serving, knowing, and loving God and our neighbor. So to obey the laws of our Creator is not only to honor him but also to honor our own design, just as a fish does when it lives in the water rather than on land or the way a car owner does when she follows the owner's manual.

In this community there is also the *moral sourcebook*, the Bible. The book of Deuteronomy is a series of sermons by Moses for the community of God's people. The divinely revealed Ten Commandments are laid out in chapter 5, and then in chapter 6 Moses says that it is "these commandments" that "are to be on your hearts" and impressed on your children. The Christian church, of course, has more than

Deuteronomy—it has the entire Bible as its sourcebook for practical moral wisdom.

In this community there is also what Hunter calls *moral discourse.* It is not sufficient to put the moral rules up on the whiteboard and have students memorize them. As the chapter says, you must "talk about them when you sit at home and when you walk along the road, when you lie down and when you get up" (verse 7). Applying the rules to concrete daily life takes much wisdom and constant attention. We must look at the numerous choices we make every day and ask: "What is the right thing to do in this situation?" You must talk to your children about why a particular decision or action that day fits in with what we know of Jesus and his gospel. We have to show children that God's commands are not just something you believe in the abstract but are to be "on your hands and . . . on your foreheads" (verse 8). We are to show how your daily thoughts ("foreheads") and actions ("hands") are shaped by your faith and experience of Christ.

In this community there is *moral imagination*. Alasdair MacIntyre's classic *After Virtue* shows that moral character has for centuries been instilled most powerfully by stories that embody and illustrate moral qualities.[12] Stories from our own community's past can be most formative of all.

> In the future, when your son asks you,
> "What is the meaning of the stipulations,
> decrees and laws the LORD our God has
> commanded you?" tell him: "We were
> slaves of Pharaoh in Egypt, but the LORD
> brought us out of Egypt with a mighty

hand. Before our eyes the LORD sent signs and wonders—great and terrible—on Egypt and Pharaoh and his whole household. But he brought us out from there to bring us in and give us the land he promised on oath to our ancestors. The LORD commanded us to obey all these decrees and to fear the LORD our God, so that we might always prosper and be kept alive, as is the case today." (Deuteronomy 6:20–24)

Notice that when children ask the big "why" question—as in "*Why* must we never lie? Never steal? Never commit adultery?"—they are not to get a lecture on moral philosophy. They are given narratives—stories of struggles between good and evil—that capture imaginations and shape hearts even more than arguments and propositions.

Hebrews 11 gives us a New Testament summary of what we might call "heroes of faith," including Abraham, Jacob, Joseph, Moses, and others. But it is important to realize that these biblical figures are not like the moral exemplars of other cultures. Abraham, Jacob, David, Peter—just to take four—were deeply flawed and had lives marked by repeated, serious moral failures. Why are these the stories we get to give our children?

It is because the gospel is the message of salvation by God's unmerited grace. Christ's salvation is not for the strong and competent and accomplished, but for those strong enough to admit they are none of these things. Instead of a series of triumphant, nearly flawless paragons of virtue, the Bible points us to weak people who don't deserve God's grace, don't seek it, and don't appreciate it even after God has given it to them anyway. The greatest recipients of grace are the biggest repenters. It is stories such as these that get across so vividly the principles and power of the gospel. Christian moral principles are dynamic implications of Jesus's saving love for us in the gospel. Doing justice, being honest, reconciling with enemies, and staying chaste are things we will *want* to do if the gospel of Jesus's costly grace is not only understood but grasped with the heart and applied to daily life.

Finally, a Christian community that is a moral ecology is characterized by *moral modeling*. In the midst of all the instructions about what we should be doing with our children, Moses says:

> Be sure to keep the commands of the LORD your God and the stipulations and decrees he has given you. Do what is

right and good in the LORD's sight.
(Deuteronomy 6:17–18)

Here is perhaps the most commonsense feature of
an effective, character-forming community. Children have to see gospel-based moral values and
traits actually embodied in the people around
them. We must live what we believe and profess.
Hypocrisy will alienate our children from us, and
if it does, we will deserve it.

Kathy and I gratefully discovered that despite our mediocre parenting, our young teen-
age sons grew up with a very positive regard for
the Christian faith. It was because they were
surrounded in our New York City church with
young men and women in their twenties and
early thirties who were accomplished in their
fields and attractive in their character, but also
deeply committed believers.

Modern parenting manuals often counsel that parents not try to instill their own "values" in children but instead support them in forming their own.[13] But the fact remains that everyone else in the world—from advertisers to social media platforms to most of your child's schoolteachers—will implicitly or overtly be trying to catechize your children with its ideas such as "live your own truth." If you don't teach your children well, someone else will. If we don't form moral ecologies that shape our children into Christ-likeness, they will be shaped by the world's moral ecology.

Enduring the Sword

When Mary and Joseph took Jesus to the temple for his dedication, they met an old man,

Simeon, who by the Holy Spirit was able to discern that this child was the Messiah long promised. After his famous exclamation, "You may now dismiss your servant in peace. For my eyes have seen your salvation" (Luke 2:29–30), he then turned to Mary and prophesied:

> This child is destined to cause the falling and rising of many in Israel, and to be a sign that will be spoken against, so that the thoughts of many hearts will be revealed. And a sword will pierce your own soul too. (Luke 2:34–35)

Simeon is saying that for all the peace that Jesus will bring into the world, he will also bring conflict. His claim to be the Son of God will bring salvation and rest to many people, but others will reject it and so people will be divided over him.

And Mary in particular, as Jesus's mother, will experience both the profoundest joy at seeing the greatness of her son *and* the deepest grief as she watches his arrest, torture, and death. Of course on the far side of Jesus's resurrection it would become clear to Mary that what her son endured was for the salvation of us all. But up until that moment, her experience was not very different from what mothers, and indeed all parents, experience. Amidst the joy—a sword.

In a sense every love relationship brings "a sword in the heart," because when you love someone truly you bind your heart to the other person with the result that your happiness is tied to his or her happiness. You can't be fully happy when they are not. This heart-tying is involuntary in the case of parents, so that, as it has been said, "you can be only as happy as your unhappiest child."[14]

No wonder so many modern people have given parenting a pass. But just as Jesus could not bless the world without the suffering of his parents, so we cannot give the world the blessing of our children's new life without accepting the sword in our hearts. We should bear that sword with extraordinary prayer rather than self-pity and worry (Philippians 4:6), but also with the knowledge that Jesus himself gave us the blessing of his salvation at unimaginable cost—and with literal nails and thorns.

This is a great resource that Christianity provides to parents. It is the example of Christ, who shows us that to nurture life always takes sacrifice. Those who wish to see civilization continue and love increase welcome the sacrifices that come with new life. This book is addressed to them.

If you give your children to God, cultivate their hearts in community, and accept the sacrifices of parenting with prayer and grace, your children may find themselves contemplating the second "new" birth by the Holy Spirit. To that we turn in the next two chapters.

Second Birth

Now there was a man of the Pharisees named Nicodemus, a member of the Jewish ruling council. He came to Jesus at night and said, "Rabbi, we know you are a teacher who has come from God. For no one could perform the miraculous signs you are doing if God were not with him."

In reply Jesus declared, "I tell you the truth, no one can see the kingdom of God unless he is born again."

"How can a man be born when he is old?" Nicodemus asked. "Surely he cannot enter a second time into his mother's womb to be born!"

Jesus answered, "I tell you the truth, no one can enter the kingdom of God unless he is born of water and the Spirit. Flesh gives birth to flesh, but the Spirit gives birth to spirit."

—JOHN 3:1-6

This is the most famous and substantial text in the Bible telling us about the "second" or new birth. Let's ask this passage several questions about being born again. Who is it for? Where is it from? What does it do? How does it come?

Who Is It For?

What does the average American think when they hear the term "born-again" Christian? They usually think of a particular type of person. People know that some folks are more emotional, they seek a cathartic experience and want to raise their hands and sway as they sing their hymns. Fine, they think, that's the type of person who likes born-again religion.

Others may think of people who need a lot of moral structure. They may have had broken lives, having fallen into addiction or other kinds of life-dominating problems. This sort, it is often said, may benefit from a regimented, structured kind of religion with lots of absolutes and rules. That's another kind of person who needs born-again religion.

Finally, in our society, "born-again" Christians have a reputation for voting for politically conservative candidates. The reality is certainly more complex, but the public image leads to the same kind of conclusion. To be born again, it is thought, is something only for a person of a certain temperament, life experience, or brand of politics.

The trouble with this whole view is seen in Nicodemus himself. This chapter in the gospel of John gives us an account of a man who comes to speak to Jesus at night. We are told a lot about him in two brief phrases. He was "a man of the Pharisees" and "a member of the Jewish ruling council," known as the Sanhedrin. From these two facts we can deduce a number of things about him. As a member of the council he would have been an older male of the ruling class. As a Pharisee he would have been not only moral and religious, but highly self-disciplined.

He was not, then, an "emotional type." Nor was he someone whose life had collapsed and who needed more moral structure in his life. He was a Pharisee—the very epitome of moral structure.

Was he, however, a superconservative type? You might think so, but consider his startling portrayal here. He is at the heart of the establishment, a gatekeeper of the leading cultural institutions of his day. Yet here we see him coming to Jesus—a man who had never gone to the rabbinical schools, who had no academic or political credentials, and who came from the lower rungs of the working class. Yet Nicodemus respectfully calls him "Rabbi," and seeks to learn from him. This shows not only enormous generosity of spirit but also an unusual open-mindedness.

So who is Nicodemus? He's a moral, successful person, but also as open-minded, tolerant, and generous a man as you could hope to find. He is neither a broken person who needs structure, nor an emotional person who needs a cathartic experience, nor someone of a prejudiced, conservative temperament. And yet it is to *him* that Jesus says, "You must be born again."

He does not say, "You know, Nicodemus, you are a pretty good man in many ways. You have a lot to your credit, but if you just add these practices and these duties you can be right with God." No, the message is that nothing he has done so far has actually moved him any closer to God at all. Jesus says, "If you want a relationship with the King of the world you have to be completely remade from the ground up. You must be born again."

Jesus's call cannot, therefore, be a call to dysfunctional people to adopt structured morality and religion. It's actually a *challenge* to morality and religion, because that's what Nicodemus represents. Jesus is subverting the patronizing idea that the new birth is only for a certain type of person. And if salvation is based on the new birth and not on attainments, then anyone can be born again.

Jesus's point is radical but simple. Everyone needs to be born again because no one can even see the kingdom of God without it. That's who the new birth is for. It's for everyone.

Where Is It From?

In John 3:3 Jesus says you have to be born again
to see the kingdom of God, and in verse 5 he
says you must be born again to enter the kingdom of God.[1]

Remember that Jesus is speaking to a Jewish
Pharisee. What would the "kingdom of God"
have meant to Nicodemus? It would have meant
the resurrection at the end of time, the new heavens and new earth that Isaiah promised (Isaiah
65:17, 66:22). As a team or organization riven
with conflict and dysfunction becomes a cohe-
sive unit under a good leader, so when God returns to the earth at the end of time the presence
of his full kingly power and glory will put everything right.

Many Greek philosophers believed history was

endless and cyclical, with periodic great purges in which the world burned and was cleansed, after which history started afresh. They had a technical term for that. They called it the *palingenesia*, which means the regeneration or the rebirth of the world. But these "rebirths" were never final. They started things over, but history always inevitably moved into decline.[2]

Yet in Matthew 19:28, Jesus takes this technical Greek philosophical term and uses it in the most startling way. He speaks of "*the* renewal of all things [*palingenesia*], when the Son of Man sits on his glorious throne." He is saying that the philosophers had it wrong. When he returns to rule there will indeed be a regeneration of the world, but it will be once and for all. It will not merely wind things up in order for them to run down again, but it will destroy all evil and death and wipe away all suffering and tears.

That, of course, is an amazing claim in itself. But in Titus 3:5–6, when Paul is talking about the new birth, he says, "He saved us through the washing of regeneration and renewal by the Holy Spirit, whom he poured out on us generously through Jesus Christ our Savior." In English that is not so striking, but the Greek word for "regeneration" is *palingenesia*. So Paul is saying directly what Jesus is hinting at by tying the new birth to the kingdom of God.

Even though the kingdom of God and all its infinite power to cleanse and renew will only come fully at the end of history, the new birth is an implantation of God's future power into your life *now*. The future glory that God will show forth at the end of time to heal everything in the whole world can come into your life now, partially but actually, and begin to change you from the inside out.

So where is the new birth from? It's from the future! I'm sure you are surprised that the Bible includes a message that is more often associated with time-travel stories, but here's a piece of time-travel *non*fiction. The new birth is not a matter of us going into the future; it's the future coming into us. It's the time that's traveling, not you. It is the power of God to regenerate the world coming into your life now to begin to slowly but surely change you into the image of his Son (Romans 8:29).

That all might sound very abstract, so let me show you one very practical implication. Never underestimate the power of the new birth for change. Look at Peter—he was cowardly and spineless. Look at Paul—he was rigid, harsh, and cruel. Yet the new birth made one as coura-geous as a lion and the other like a tender shep-herd, and turned them both into world-changing figures. And were they made of more promising raw material than you or me? They were not. There is no hurt or fear, no guilt or shame, no weakness or flaw—there is nothing in your life that the new birth cannot remove and begin to heal.

What Does It Do?

The most essential feature about the new birth is what it does to the person who experiences it. From Jesus's words we learn that the new birth is, as we might expect from the metaphor, the implantation of new life.

In John 3:5 Jesus says we must be "born of water and the spirit." Many people read that as meaning we need to have two things in order to be saved: we need to have faith and to be baptized.

But it is much more likely that Jesus is talking about only one thing. Bible scholars point out that Jesus is referring here to Ezekiel 36, in which the Spirit of God is likened to water because in arid, desert climates, water was so necessary for survival it virtually *was* life. In short, the new birth is the implantation of God's very life—the Holy Spirit himself—into you. What does that mean? There are certainly many things we could say if we would roam all over the New Testament. But we will confine ourselves to the metaphor Jesus uses here—of being born like a child out of the womb into the world. To be born again means at least two things that are implied in this image—new sensibility and new identity.

The first is that in the new birth we receive new sensibility.[3] Jesus says you need to be born again to "see" the kingdom (verse 3).

All living things, even plants, have some way

to sense their environment. Human beings, of course, have their five senses, and when a child is born she is bombarded with new sensory experiences of light, sound, feeling, smelling, and tasting. It must be overwhelming.

In a similar way, the new birth brings a new spiritual sense. It is the ability not only to intellectually grasp truths about God, yourself, and the world that never made sense before, but also to feel those truths in your heart in a completely new way. To be spiritually alive means you can sense spiritual realities because now you have spiritual sight and taste. One of the very first places this change becomes obvious is in how you read the Bible. You may have been raised going to church and Sunday school and have known various Bible stories and even memorized many verses. But after the new birth, you start to see connections and truths in the Bible that you never noticed or that you may have assented to mentally, that now move, comfort, and illuminate you in ways you had never experienced before.

You had heard "God loves you" or "God is holy and just" or "God watches over you," and you may have agreed with some of them as propositions, but now they become life-transforming realities that shape your daily life and actions. You begin to see implications you never dreamed of. "Wait!" you may say. "If this is true about God—then why do I feel like this? Why do I behave like that? I don't have to be like this anymore." Archibald Alexander, the first teacher of theology at Princeton Theological Seminary in the early 1800s, speaks about it this way:

> Every man, on whom this divine operation has passed, experiences *new views*

of divine truth. The soul sees, in these things, *that* which it never saw before. It discerns, in the truth of God, a beauty and excellence, of which it had no conception until now.

Alexander very quickly insists that, even though this new spiritual "sense and sensibility" is true of all who experience the new birth, we must not expect that it dawns and develops identically in each person. He writes: "Whatever may be the diversity in the clearness of the views of different persons, or in the particular truths brought before the mind, they all agree in this—that there is a new perception of truth."[4] No one can insist that these new perceptions come in the same way. Sometimes the change may be dramatic, sometimes very gradual. Also, it is not this or that particular truth that always comes home to the newborn person. This new spiritual sense can operate in an enormous variety of ways.

Still, there are some commonalities. One of them is to hear believers say, "I'd heard this all my life, but it never made sense before." In particular, people declare that Jesus's love in dying on the Cross for them has finally become palpable, melting, and beautiful. "Like newborn babies long for the pure milk of the Word,"[5] writes the apostle Peter in 1 Peter 2:2. Biblical truths go from being words on a page to being food and drink that you relish and that become part of you.

Here's a striking example. Years ago I was in a committee of ministers that was examining young men who were going into ministry. We asked each of them to tell us something of how they had come to faith in Christ. One after the other said something like this: "I was raised in the church, but I never heard there the gospel preached that you are saved by sheer grace." They then went on to explain how they had finally heard the gospel through some other ministry. At one point, after one more candidate had said the same thing, one of the senior ministers in the room told a story.

He said that he too had been raised in the church and at one point had even tried to study Christianity by taking some educational courses, including one in which he had to learn about Martin Luther and read excerpts from his famous commentary on Galatians. A couple of years later, when he was in the military, a chaplain explained the gospel to him. He realized that he had always thought being a Christian was trying to live like Jesus, and if we did that with sufficient sincerity and diligence, we would go to heaven. But now the chaplain explained that salvation was by sheer grace through Christ's work on our behalf—his life, death, and resurrection—and our salvation could be received once and for all in an act of faith. Gratefully and joyfully he took that step of faith with the chaplain.

Then he asked the chaplain why no one had ever told him the gospel before. "And," he added, "I don't know why Martin Luther didn't know the gospel."

The chaplain looked puzzled and asked him why he would say that. He replied, "Well, I read his book on Galatians and I didn't see it in there." The chaplain quietly suggested that he go back and reread the book.

"I did," he said, "and there on nearly every page—underlined and highlighted by me—there was the gospel." He hadn't been able to see it—his spiritual eyes had not been open. He concluded his story: "Right now there are people in my congregation, under my preaching, who are not hearing the gospel—because at this point they still do not have 'ears to hear' that come with the new birth."

New Identity

Besides a new spiritual sight and sense, the new birth brings a new identity. That fits with the metaphor of a new birth. To be born as a child is to be born into a family and to receive a name. So John 1:12–13 says:

> Yet to all who did receive him, to those who believed in his name, he gave the right to become children of God—children born not of natural descent,

nor of human decision or a husband's
will, but born of God. (John 1:12–13)

To be "born of God" is no longer to have a name
or identity based on either "natural descent"—the
social status or family pedigree of the traditional
culture—or "human decision"—the achievement
and performance of the modern meritocracy. Instead it is to have the "rights" and privileges of
being God's child. It's a new sense of self and
worth based on God's fatherly love and his identi-
fication with us, all secured by Christ's work, not
ours. That is what we are born into when we are
born again.

What does that mean practically?

To be "born again" means not to become just
an improved person but a new one. Paul writes
that if anyone is "in Christ" he or she is a "new

creation" (2 Corinthians 5:17). He does not mean that literally everything about us changes when we are born again. Rather something radically new comes in, and everything that has been within us changes places, as it were, and is reconfigured.

In a famous passage Paul says that "in Christ" there is no Jew or Greek, male or female, slave or free, for all are "one in Christ" (Galatians 3:28), and yet that does not mean these distinctions are obliterated. New Testament scholar Larry Hurtado writes:

> [Christians'] . . . ethnic, social, and gender distinctions are to be regarded as relativized radically, [for] all believers of whatever ethnic, sexual, or social class are now "one in Christ Jesus." But . . .

Paul did not treat these distinctions as actually effaced. So for example . . . he persisted in referring to himself proudly as a member of his ancestral people, a "Hebrew" and an "Israelite" . . . but he also insisted that "in Christ" . . . these distinctions were no longer to be regarded as *defining* believers in the ways that they had functioned before.[6]

The "newness," then, of the new birth is not that all the various features of your life—your gender, nationality, social class, and so on— pass away. Rather, none of them function any longer as your chief identity factor. They no longer serve as your main significance and security, or as the main makers of your self-regard and self-definition. With one person her nationality ("I'm Irish") might be less of an identity factor than her vocation ("I'm a successful lawyer"). But for another Irish lawyer, it is the nationality that is a greater source of pride and meaning, and so he feels more solidarity with others of his nationality than of his profession. For a third person it is her social activism that is her main meaning in life, and so she feels more unity and pride not in others of her nationality or vocation but with those of her politics and justice work.

In every case, however, there is something that we are most proud of, something that enables us to feel confident that we are good people, that our lives are justified. In Christ, this is what changes. All other identity factors are matters of performance or pedigree, and they not only make us insecure, lest we not live up to the standards of our pursuit, but they also tend to make us tribal and cold toward those who do not share our identity.

The gospel, however, is radically different. First, it gives us a unique, transformative new self-understanding. It tells us we are so lost and incapable of pleasing God that Jesus had to die for us, but we are so loved that he was glad to die for us. On the Cross our sins were put on him—he was treated as our life record deserves—so that if we put our faith in him, we receive his righteousness; that is, we are treated as Jesus's life record deserves (2 Corinthians 5:21). God now loves us "in Christ," as if we had done all he has done. He loves us "even as" he loves his Son (John 17:23). That becomes the deepest foundation of our identity, meaning, and self-view, demoting but not removing all the other things that are true of us.

At first one might think that this would just make Christians one more tribe who looked down on those without their truth, but that is to forget what that gospel truth is. The gospel says we are deserving of death but saved by sheer grace. The only people who are saved are those who finally admit they are not spiritually or morally better than anyone else. However, salvation by grace does not only humble—it lifts us up at the same time. James 1:9–10 says that Christians who are economically poor "should take pride in their high position," but believers who are rich or well off "should take pride in their humiliation." Let's unpack that a little.

Ordinary identity is either up or down, depending on performance. If your deepest pride is found in your ethnicity or family, then the performance of others in your tribe—or of you yourself—will bring either honor or shame to the whole. There will be times you are bursting with pride and other times you will be humiliated. If your identity is the traditional Western one based on your individual achievements, you will again be either up or down.

But the Christian who has embraced the gospel has received a message that we are sinful and in ourselves worthy of condemnation, yet loved perfectly and unconditionally in Christ and free from condemnation (Romans 8:1). That means we always have a low position *and* an even greater high position in our minds at the same time. James points out that, at various times and in various situations, it is good for Christians to dwell more on one of those truths than the other. If you are poor and have been told all your life you are worthless, then the high position that comes with the gospel should be meditated on constantly in order to heal your soul. But if you are successful and have been getting accolades all your live, then you should think long and often about the low position that comes with the gospel.

This new identity, then, really is a "new creation" that changes everything. It changes our attitude toward people of other races and classes—no longer does our own race or status so dominate our identity that we look down on anyone. Our new "low" position enables us to listen to and learn from people we previously would have despised. But our new "high" position enables us to take on challenges or to speak out and go up against wrongdoing or to testify to our Christian faith—all in ways that previously we would never have had the inner strength to attempt or even the desire to do.

How does the new birth actually bring about this shift? The first feature—new sight and sensibility—is crucial to this second one of identity. If a lonely and unhappy child in an orphanage is simply told he has been adopted by a wonderful family, that won't change him. He has to meet them, be hugged by them, be loved and cared for by them day in and day out. Only then will the legal change in his name be translated into a new inner happiness and security.

In the same way, the moment we put our faith in Christ, we become legally children of God (John 1:12–13). But that will not reconfigure our hearts and our actual functional identity unless, through the new presence of God's Spirit, we actually sense his love, holiness, glory, and reality. Paul says that when we give our lives to Christ, the Spirit of God comes into our heart, "and by him we cry . . . 'Father.' The Spirit himself testifies with our spirit that we are God's children" (Romans 8:15–16). As we participate

in ordinary Christian practices—of reading the
Bible and hearing it preached, of individual and
corporate prayer, of building each other up in
Christian community, of participating in baptism and the Lord's Supper—the Spirit makes
our new identity real to our hearts and we
change, slowly but surely. Put in the language
of Saint Augustine, the new birth begins to "re-
order your loves." You don't love your family or
career or people less, but by the power of the
Holy Spirit you learn to value God's love more
and more.

When I was a young pastor I remember counseling a woman whose life had been changed by
the gospel. As she told me her story, she could remember at least four different stages in her life.
When she was a young girl growing up in a very
strict church, she said to herself, "I know I'm
somebody special because I'm more moral than

all my friends." The trouble was, of course, that when she slipped up in her behavior, she hated herself because the very basis of her self-worth was disintegrating. Then she moved into a stage of life in which she said to herself, "I know I'm somebody special because this great guy loves me." If anything, her instability increased. She said, "Not only was I emotionally high or devastated depending on whether I was noticed by men, but I stayed in relationships I should have broken off but I was afraid to."

After several years she found some friends who rightly chastised her for taking her identity and happiness from male attention and romance. But then they added that her self-worth should be based instead on her having her own career. She embraced their counsel, working hard on her education and career. Now she said to herself, "I'm somebody because I am a successful person, making good money, and accomplishing things in the world." But she added, "Now I found whenever I had a bump in my career path that it just destroyed me the way the romantic bumps used to destroy me."

Then somebody came along to her and said, "Oh, you don't need all that to know you're somebody. You just need to know you are a good, kind person who helps others." And she said, "I threw myself into helping. I threw myself into volunteer work. I threw myself into listening to anybody who had a problem. I threw myself into trying to help emotionally needy people get better, until I was so tired. And I hated myself because I was supposed to love these people, and I didn't even like them."

In her identity shifts, she went from "I'm somebody because I'm moral—because I'm beautiful—because I'm successful—because I'm helpful," until she finally realized that in every case she was trying to save herself, and she was exhausted. She said, "I realized what I really needed was to know God loved me because he loved me and because of what Jesus had done. That changed everything."

The new birth is not, "I've got weak self-esteem and I need a boost from God." The new birth isn't a sort of vitamin supplement that adds the vague idea of "God's love" to the mix of all the things through which you are achieving your self-worth. Being born again not only changes *what* you look to as your highest good but *how* you look to it. Your heart rests in Christ's freely offered love for you—it does not work for it. It's an identity based on an entirely new foundation.

There is a story (probably a legend) about Saint Augustine. He was converted after having had many relationships with women. One day he was walking and one of his old mistresses came up to greet him. He was perfectly courteous but somewhat distant. She was puzzled. As he politely said good-bye and began to walk on, she said, "Augustine! You know it's me, don't you?" He turned with a smile and said, "I know, but it is not me." Things that had mattered the most to him no longer drove and mastered him. He had a new inner fullness instead of needy emptiness. He had been born again.

How Does It Come?

I've been talking about conversion—turning to God in faith—and the new birth as if they were the same thing. Theologians over the years have made a helpful distinction here. In one sense these two things might be said to be two sides of the same coin, because they always come together. Jesus says in Matthew 18:3 that "unless you are converted . . . you will not enter the kingdom of God,"[7] and in John 3 that unless you are "born of the Spirit" you cannot enter the kingdom of God. If both are absolutely necessary, then it follows that no one is truly a Christian, a citizen of God's kingdom and a child in his family, unless both happen.

But while the Bible constantly tells us to put our faith in God, it nowhere tells us to give ourselves the new birth. How could we? That violates the metaphor. The regeneration of the heart, the implantation of the Holy Spirit, is not something you can do any more than a baby can decide to be conceived and born. And yet turning to God in faith *is* something we are called to do. Conversion is what you and I do to come to God, but the new birth is what God does within us.

So the real question is—how do we turn to God so we can be born again? There are two parts, and they are implied here. The first one has to do with grace. The second one has to do with Christ himself.

First, we must turn away from our sins and efforts to save ourselves. Jesus says to Nicodemus in John 3, "You must be born again." Then in John 4, we're given a great example of Jesus calling a woman to conversion, a woman who is the exact opposite of Nicodemus. It's not just that he's a male and she's a female. The point is, her life has been a complete ruin and his life has been a complete success in the world's terms, and yet Jesus calls them both to be saved by grace, as a gift.

When we moved to New York in the late 1980s, Manhattan was a much different place than it is now. Once a month I used to speak at a breakfast at the Harvard Club, and when I'd come up from the F train on Sixth Avenue there were prostitutes and drug dealers around. Then I would walk into the Harvard Club, filled with wood-paneled rooms, overstuffed leather chairs, roaring fires, and everyone looking prosperous and pulled together (and quite a few of them actually were). But the gospel told me then and now that the Nicodemuses in the Harvard Club and the Samaritan women out on the sidewalk were equally disqualified from any salvation based on performance yet equally qualified for salvation based on grace.

The message is this: no matter how good and well-ordered your life is, you *must* be born again, yet no matter how chaotic your life has been or how often and profoundly you have failed, you *can* be born again. Jesus is saying, "You're all on the same level. The most accomplished person and the person whose life seems to be the biggest failure come to God as equals. You are in the same spot. You need to be, and can be, born again." Nicodemus had been trying to save himself with his morality and accomplishments and therefore had been playing God, trying to be his own savior. The woman at the well in John 4 is revealed to have been seeking joy and satisfaction in a series of broken romantic relationships and marriage. She was trying to do the same thing. Yes, it was in a way that brought her social opprobrium, while Nicodemus's way brought him social honor. But in God's eyes, whether you try to save yourself by being moral, or helpful, or beautiful, it doesn't matter. You're trying to save yourself. You're putting yourself in the place of God.

Therefore, everybody—the apparently "best" and "worst"—stands at the same place and on the same level in their need of the grace of God. Babies do not contribute anything to their conception and birth. They don't bring themselves about. They don't get born because they've planned on it. It all has to do with what the parents have done. It has nothing to do with what they do.

Paradoxically, you must understand you can contribute nothing to your salvation in order to receive it. As long as you think "I can save myself. I'm really a good enough person," you are still spiritually blind. You can't see the kingdom of God or experience his grace. This is called repentance—and it's not simply being sorry for this or that sin. This is what the Bible calls "repentance unto life" (Acts 18:11). The first thing you have to do to be converted is to repent before God's grace and say, "I see I've been trying to save myself, and I need your free grace."

The most famous example of this is Martin Luther himself. Here's what he said happened as he was getting converted: "I labored diligently and anxiously as to how to understand Paul's word in Romans 1:17." He was struggling over a verse, "where he says that the righteousness of God is revealed in the gospel." Finally, he says, "I grasped that the righteousness of God is that righteousness which through grace and sheer mercy God gives us by faith. Thereupon I felt myself to be reborn and to have gone through open doors into paradise . . . When I saw the difference, that law is one thing and the gospel is another, I broke through."[8]

There it is. Luther felt like he had been struck with a lightning bolt. For years he knew that he should repent of his sins and get God's forgiveness, but then he thought that he was on his own to pull himself together and give God a righteous life in order to get his blessing and favor. Suddenly he realized not only that he had done sins and bad deeds but that even his good deeds had been done for the wrong reasons—in order to control what God and others thought of him, in order to create an identity for himself of being a good person, in order to save himself and play God. It was when he not only repented for his bad deeds but also for the reason he had been doing all his good deeds that he felt himself "to be reborn." When he realized the difference between the gospel and saving himself through moral effort—he "broke through."

The Beauty of Jesus

So the first thing we must do to be converted is to turn away from our self-salvation schemes in repentance. But then we must turn toward Jesus in faith, seeing the beauty of what Christ has done. It's not enough just to believe in the grace of God in general; you have to have faith in what Jesus Christ has done in particular.

I saw all three of my sons being born, and with each child it was different. They were squalling or silent, kicking or almost motionless. But they all had one thing in common. They were not being born, getting their new life, or being brought into the world by *their* labor. They were being brought into the world through the pain and labor of their mother. We live today in a society in which giving birth is not as painful or life threatening as it used to be. But when Jesus was talking about being born again he was living in a time in which you did not see the light of life unless someone loved you enough not only to experience pain and suffering for you but also to put her very life on the line. Indeed, in those days, many people were brought to life through their mother's death.

That's the reason Jesus later on in the Gospel of John makes a remarkable comparison. In John 16:16 he says, "In a little while you will see me no more," referring to his death on the Cross. Then immediately he says, "A woman giving birth to a child has pain because her hour has come; but when her baby is born she forgets the anguish because of her joy that a child is born into the world" (John 16:23).

Why, when he is talking about his death, does he suddenly bring up a woman in labor? And why does he speak of the painful moment of giving birth as her "hour"? Students of the Gospel of John know that whenever Jesus talks about his death on the Cross he calls it his "hour."[9]

See what Jesus is saying? "Your first birth brings you physical life because someone risked her life, but your second birth brings you spiritual and eternal life because someone gave his life. That someone was me." And if we stay with Jesus's metaphor in John 16 it gets even more wonderful. He says that, in spite of her incredible pain, a new mother is filled with joy at the sight of her child. So Jesus has the audacity to say, "That's just a dim hint of the joy I sense when I look at you. All my suffering, torment, and death I have willingly borne, for the greater joy of saving and loving you." Until you see that and believe and rest in that, you cannot be born again.

Growing in Grace

Simon Peter, a servant and apostle of Jesus Christ: To those who through the righteousness of our God and Savior Jesus Christ have received a faith as precious as ours . . . His divine power has given us everything we need for a godly life . . . He has given us his very great and precious promises so that through them you may participate in the divine nature . . . For this very reason, make every effort to add to your faith goodness; and to goodness, knowledge; and to knowledge, self-control; and to self-control, perseverance; and to perseverance, godliness; and to godliness, mutual affection; and to mutual affection, love. For if you possess these qualities in increasing measure, they will keep you from being ineffective and unproductive in your knowledge of our Lord Jesus Christ. But whoever does not have them is nearsighted and blind, forgetting that they have been cleansed from their past sins.

—2 PETER 1:1, 3–9

But grow in the grace and knowledge of our Lord and Savior Jesus Christ. To him be glory both now and forever!

—2 PETER 3:18

Jesus's image of salvation as a new birth was taken up by the other New Testament writers, by Paul (Titus 3:5), James (James 1:8), John (1 John 5:1), and Peter as well. Twice in his first letter Peter tells Christians they have been born again (1 Peter 1:3, 23). One of the clearest implications of this birth metaphor must not be overlooked. Human beings do not, like the goddess Athena in the Greek legend, spring to life full grown from the forehead of Zeus. We begin as the tiniest, most helpless babies. The contrast of our newborn selves with our full-grown selves could not be greater. The amount of growth that a newborn must undergo is staggering—he or she must double their size in the first four to six months.

Do newborn Christians, however, evidence anything like that kind of change and transformation? The groundwork for it has been laid, as we have seen. We have the indwelling of God's Spirit. But do we grow?

In Peter's second letter he proceeds to talk about spiritual growth. In both the opening verses and his concluding statement he urges us to "grow in grace."

Growth in Grace Is Possible

Remember who is writing this book—"Simon Peter, a servant and apostle of Jesus Christ" (2

Peter 1:1). Peter was an apostle who lived with Jesus. He saw Christ transfigured on the mountain. He heard the voice of the Father coming out of heaven. He failed Jesus, but then Jesus forgave, healed, and commissioned him to be a leader in his movement. Then, after his resurrection, with the nail prints still visible, Jesus trained Peter personally.

Imagine all that happening to you. We throw the word "life-changing" around too lightly in our culture, but certainly if you had personally seen the transfiguration and the resurrection *that* would have transformed your entire life. But then look what Peter says: "Simon Peter, a servant and apostle of Jesus Christ, to those who through the righteousness of our God and Savior Jesus Christ have received a faith as precious as ours." The Greek word used there, *isotimon,* means "of equal merit and value." How remarkable it is that he writes to Christians hundreds of miles away and many decades after these events that he saw with his own eyes, yet he says that their faith is of equal life-changing value as his. He is saying, "Your life can be as revolutionized by the gospel of Jesus Christ as mine was."

How could that be? Almost immediately Peter explains. Verse 4 tells us that through the "precious" promises (the same word)—the promises of the gospel—we "participate in the divine nature." When we receive the Holy Spirit through the new birth, we get God's DNA, as it were. That does not mean that somehow we mystically merge with our deity, but it means that the love, wisdom, truthfulness, justice, mercy, and goodness of God is instilled in us. The

Holy Spirit connects you to the spiritual character of God the way your DNA connects you to the physical character of your ancestors.

In the end, it was not the eyewitness experiences that changed the apostles. Remember that Judas lived with Jesus, saw the beauty of his person and his great miracles, but still turned away. Even when the resurrected Jesus appeared to his disciples on a mountain in Galilee, some worshipped but "some doubted" (Matthew 28:17). What truly changed them was the same thing that all Christians have, the indwelling of the Holy Spirit (Acts 1:8).

When the Bible calls you to grow in grace, it is very different than saying, "Be virtuous." Many have thought that the New Testament is simply calling everybody in general to base their lives on the ethical model of Jesus. Jesus was a man who did love and mercy and justice, they say. If we all lived like him, the world would be a better place.

With all due respect to the sentiment, the biblical authors are not that naïve and foolish. To call people to live like Christ, to adopt a way of life that goes utterly against our nature through an act of the will, is to ask for the impossible. The Bible's calls to Christians to become like Christ assume they've been born again and they are a partaker of the divine nature. When New Testament writers say, "Love your neighbor as yourself," they're saying, "Nurture that new nature inside you so you can love your neighbor as yourself." You have to be born in order to grow. If you're going to grow physically, you have to be born physically. If you're going to grow spiritually, you have to be born spiritually.

There is no excuse for not having a radically

changed life if you're a Christian. Have you
given up on change in certain areas? Learned to
live with bad habits and patterns in your life?
Have you silently made peace with wrong attitudes, fears, and resentments in your heart?
You have "everything you need" for a godly life
(verse 3). Growth in grace is now a powerful
possibility.

Growth in Grace Is Gradual

Peter speaks about "adding" to your faith one
quality after another—goodness, knowledge, self-
control, mutual affection—and then says that
these must be present in "increasing measure." In
other words, growth in grace is gradual.

Our culture trains us to be impatient. A company that can only deliver the product two days

from now will be put out of business by one that
provides next-day delivery. A computer that takes
ten seconds to download something will be put
out of business by one that gives us the same
features but downloads in two seconds. Bank-
ruptcy over an eight-second difference! That's
the kind of culture we live in.

And the church often has been overly shaped
by the culture at this very point. Many churches
and ministries say directly, or at least hint implicitly, that if you really give your life to Christ
and come into our congregation and use our
methods of spiritual growth, you will be soon
delivered from anything that enslaves or ails
you. They promise spiritual victory over your
problems as a kind of magic bullet.

But the Bible never talks like that. We are born
again—we start out as spiritual babes, as Peter
says elsewhere in his letters (1 Peter 2:2). No one

goes from being an infant to a functioning adult in a few weeks, or months. It takes years and years of nurture and effort and trial and error—usually very big errors—and learning from everything. The Bible never says (to paraphrase 1 Peter 2:2): "Like newborn babies, drink in the spiritual milk of the Word of God so you may grow up in your salvation. And if you drink really, really, really hard, you'll grow up faster." No, babies grow as they grow. It takes a long time.

And yet. If you take an acorn and you try to smash a giant slab of concrete with it, the acorn will be dashed to bits. But let's imagine that slab of concrete is part of a sidewalk. Plant that acorn in the ground underneath the sidewalk. If it germinates it may find a way to sprout up and slowly, over the years, push that concrete slab aside. It may even crack it in half. That's the power of slow but steady growth.

So growth in grace is less like a bullet and more like an acorn. It comes into your life and if you water it and nurture it, it eventually will utterly change you. If the power of God is in you, it eventually will deal with your greatest weaknesses. If the love of God is in you, eventually it will confront your selfishness. But it is gradual.

It should be kept in mind that, just as growing children do, spiritually growing Christians will show many individual differences. Parents who have more than one child know that they do not all learn their first words, take their first steps, or do anything else at the same age, at the same time, and at the same rate. Even twins differ! And so it is with spiritual growth. Some of us come into God's family having had far more difficulties, mistreatment, and character challenges than others. Some of us also come with little or no knowledge of the Bible or Christian teaching while others come with a great deal, and therefore progress in the Christian life, while always gradual, progresses at different paces for different people.

There is one more way that spiritual growth follows the pattern of a child's growth into adulthood. The great eighteenth-century hymn writer John Newton (the author of "Amazing Grace") was also a wise pastor. In letters to a friend, he spoke of three basic stages of spiritual growth, which roughly corresponded to childhood, adolescence, and adulthood.[1]

Like children, new believers are often enthusiastic and filled with wonderful new feelings of both freedom from guilt and closeness to God. But, Newton says, while they have believed the gospel—that God's forgiveness is a free gift, not earned or deserved—they have not yet learned

to apply the gospel to their whole lives. They
still are, at root, legalists. They know God has
forgiven them, but now they ground their confidence that he continues to love them in their
avoidance of major sins, in their faithfulness in
prayer and growth in Christian knowledge, and
especially in their feelings of nearness to God.
All these things serve as the *basis* for their certainty that God loves them instead of the *result*
of their certainty that God loves them. Because
of this there are currents of anxiety ("Does
God really love me?") and pride ("I've given my
life to Christ—unlike these stubborn people").
Young Christians become overly downcast over
negative feelings and spiritual failures because
their feelings and spiritual successes have functioned as their "merit-causes," the basis for their
favor with God.

Therefore, Newton notices, God often allows

a period in which many things go wrong in the Christian's life. This corresponds roughly to adolescence, because adolescents can struggle with parental authority. When the spiritual feelings recede and life is going poorly, the "adolescent" Christian veers back and forth between anger at God and anger at himself or herself. But, Newton writes: "By these changing dispensations, the Lord is training him up and bringing him forward."

God leads struggling believers into a deeper understanding of the gospel. Immature Christians believe that the good feelings and circumstances of their lives have been earned through the strength of their devotion to Christ. The subtle (or not so subtle) smugness and naivete is jolted out of them by difficulties and trials. They can move forward when they go deeper into the two truths of the gospel—that they are more sinful and flawed than they had believed, but that their acceptance by God is more unconditionally secure in Christ than they ever had dared hope. As Newton writes of the growing Christian: "The hour of liberty, which he longs for, is approaching, when, by a farther discovery of the glorious Gospel, it shall be given him to know his acceptance, and to rest upon the Lord's finished salvation."[2]

Finally, Newton speaks of mature "spiritually adult" Christians. Because they have grasped the gospel more deeply, they are able to handle suffering well, realizing that evil circumstances do not mean that they are being punished for their sins, or that God does not care. Also, because they now have a more radical view of God's unconditional love for them, they have the emotional strength to be far more honest about their own besetting sins rather than justifying or denying them. In this way they can under-stand themselves and overcome their character flaws as never before. Newton writes that "[the adult's] happiness and superiority to [the adolescent] lies chiefly in this, that . . . by means—such as prayer, reading and hearing the Word—he has attained clearer, deeper, and more comprehensive views of the mystery of redeeming love."[3]

Growth in Grace Is Vital

When the New Testament speaks of grace it means God's unmerited favor, his willingness to accept you not because of your works and record but because of Jesus's. In one sense, therefore, you can't grow in grace. You can't be more justi-fied and righteous in his sight. You can't be more adopted into his family. But in another sense, you can grow greatly in the influence of these truths on your heart. Your power and experience of these great privileges can increase. When that happens, and only when that happens, you have a dynamic power in your life that changes you from the inside out.

Some years ago we were on vacation and were in a fast-food restaurant, but the service was anything but fast. Our line was moving very slowly because, as we could see, the woman behind the counter was having trouble with every order. As we got closer I could tell that the reason for all the delays was that her English was very poor. She appeared to be a recent immigrant and could not understand what was being said to her. I became impatient and said to myself: "Why did the management put someone in this position without proper language skills?" But then I remembered a Bible verse I had seen that very morning in my daily reading. It was from Deuteronomy, where God was telling the Israelites to be kind to the immigrant and foreign nationals in their midst.

> And you are to love those who are aliens,
> for you yourselves were aliens in Egypt.
> (Deuteronomy 10:19)

I was caught up short. God did not say—though he could have said—"You must love and be kind to immigrants, because I say so!" That would have put pressure directly on the will. While there is nothing wrong with that, it does not create long-lasting change. But God did not frame this command in that way. He is saying to the Israelites, "Remember, I liberated you when you were aliens and slaves. Now treat immigrants and aliens as I treated you." That doesn't merely pressure the will; it changes the heart, humbling and yet building up with a remembrance of his love. That is not calling for mere ethical compliance. It requires growth in grace—having the logic of God's grace permeate your thinking and change the motives of your heart.

And of course I instantly knew that this applied to me as well. I was never a literal slave in Egypt, but as Saint Paul wrote, I too had been "excluded from citizenship" in God's kingdom and one of the "foreigners . . . without hope and without God in the world. But now in Christ Jesus you who were once far away have been brought near by the blood of Christ" (Ephesians 2:12–13). Jesus did this by losing his power and place in heaven so that I, a spiritual foreigner and outsider, could be brought in. He was excluded so I could be included. Long before any modern talk about "checking your privilege," God provided every believer with a powerful antidote to our natural tendency toward racial and class superiority.

And so as I stepped up to the counter to speak with her the thought came to me: "Lord Jesus, I too was an alien, but you brought me in at infinite cost to yourself."

When you understand grace, it begins to change your heart and it begins to nurture the new person God is growing within you. The result is real patience, real kindness, and real behavior change.

See what we mean when we say that growth in grace is vital, from the inside out, organic rather than mechanical? You can grow a pile of stones by throwing more and more stones on the pile. In the same way you can heap up Chris-

tian activities and perfect attendance at church.
You can even grow in head knowledge of Christian doctrine and biblical facts. But that is not
the same as growing wiser, deeper, happier, and
more loving.

Are you growing like a pile of stones, or are
you growing like a child becoming a mature
adult? Growth is possible. Growth is gradual.
Growth is gracious and vital.

When Growth in Grace Is Actual

What does growth in grace actually look like
when it is in progress? Archibald Alexander gives
us this list.

There will be overall progress despite occasional lapses. Our growth will be sometimes
faster and sometimes slower. It will be stronger

in one area than another. But there will be—
over time—advance.

There will be a growing unselfishness, an ability to check one's indulgences that cost other
people, especially family members, much grief.
This means the advance in your ability to control
your spending, eating, and your tongue in public. Alexander adds, interestingly, that "the counterfeit of this is an over-scrupulous conscience,
which sometimes haggles at the most innocent
gratifications."[4]

There will be sometimes a feeling of God's reality in both corporate worship and prayer, and
an increasing desire to meet with him in such
times of devotion. This certainly waxes and wanes
depending on many factors. Illness, weariness,
trials, and difficulties, or other times of heavy
busyness and activity, can lead to a decline in
what the older writers called "God's sensible

[sensed] presence." But overall there must be continual though intermittent seasons in which we commune with God in love through prayer and reading his Word. The famous hymn by William Cowper describes this:

> Sometimes a light surprises
> The Christian while he sings;
> It is the Lord who rises
> With healing in His wings;
> When comforts are declining,
> He grants the soul again
> A season of clear shining,
> To cheer it after rain.[5]

There will be an increasing love for people who are hard to love, a willingness to involve yourself in the common good of the community through loving your neighbor, and a willingness in particular to identify publicly as a believer, sharing your faith in the hopes that others can eat the same food on which you are living.

An especially strong evidence of growth in grace is when you can bear mistreatment from others by forgiving them from the heart and by desiring their welfare even as you fearlessly but humbly seek justice and the righting of any wrongs.

There will be growing reliance on the wisdom of God in the twists, turns, and circumstances of life. Romans 8:28—that God causes "all things to work together for good to those who love God"—does not claim that every individual evil thing produces some good, but it does promise that *together* all things in your life are being fitted into a pattern, mostly unseen by you, that works for your benefit and his glory. Christians who depend on this promise find that "however dark may be your horizon, or

however many difficulties environ you . . . you
have learned to live by faith. And humble con-
tentment with your condition, though it be one
of poverty and obscurity, shows that you have
profited by sitting at the feet of Jesus."[6]

Finally, a sign of growth in grace will be increasing love for other Christians, and not just
those of your particular human tribe. Sadly, the
Christian church is still divided in large part by
race and class, so it is likely that you go to
church with people of your race, educational
level, and social class. But a great sign of growth
in grace is that you discover a closer bond with
a believer of a different social status than you do
with nonbelievers of your own. This love for
other Christians, when genuine, breaks through
the barriers of politics and ideology, race and
class, that divide all other human beings.

Have you seen these kinds of changes in your

own life—this new sensibility, new identity, new habits, new loves? Slowly but surely they should be growing in and changing you.

For one of the most intriguing examples of this new creation we can return to the figure of Nicodemus, this time looking not at John, chapter 3, but what the gospel tells us about him at the very end of the book, when Jesus dies.

In John 19, when Christ's dead body was still on the Cross, Nicodemus and Joseph of Arimathea, two wealthy, successful men of the Jewish council, come and ask for the body of Jesus. Then they go to the Cross and take the body down. After that, we're told they dressed the body themselves—they prepared it for burial. They cleaned it, wiping off all the blood and filth. Then they lovingly wrapped it and put sweet-smelling spices within the burial garments. Their actions were shocking. Why?

First of all, it was a bold move, unbelievably courageous, because when the leader of a movement is being executed, you don't want to be seen as one of his followers. Indeed, all the other followers had gone into hiding, yet these two men were willing to get up and identify clearly as his disciples.

Also, it's important to know that the only people in that culture who washed and prepared a dead body for burial were women or slaves because it was considered (and it was) a foul task. Men of high rank would never do such a thing, but Joseph and Nicodemus did.

What this means is that something had changed drastically in Nicodemus. On the one hand, he was more courageous and brave than he had ever been before. And yet, on the other hand, his masculine pride was gone. He was both bolder and humbler, more courageous and more culturally flexible than he'd ever been before. Where did this redeemed masculinity come from? It came because his whole identity had been pulled up and replanted in new soil, the soil of the gospel. As we have said, the gospel takes you both lower and higher than any other belief or experience can take you. If you are saving yourself, you are bold if successful but a bit arrogant, or if you are failing, you are humble but lacking confidence. The gospel tells you that you are a hopeless sinner in yourself but in Christ saved and loved through grace. That makes you what you see here in Nicodemus and Joseph—bold and humble, strong and tender—all at once.

The paradox of the gospel is that only those who admit their complete weakness get this strong, and only those who, as it were, "lose themselves" actually "find themselves" (Matthew 10:39). C. S. Lewis ends his book *Mere Christianity* describing it.

> The principle runs through all life from top to bottom. Give up yourself, and you will find your real self. Lose your life and you will save it. Submit to death, death of your ambitions and favourite wishes every day and death of your whole body in the end: submit with every fibre of your being, and you will find eternal life. Keep back nothing. Nothing that you have not given away will ever be really yours. Nothing in you that has not died will ever be raised from the dead. Look for yourself, and you will find in the long run only hatred, loneliness, despair, rage,

ruin, and decay. But look for Christ and you will find Him, and with Him everything else thrown in.[7]

The Blessing of God

Hebrews 6:7–8 tells us that life and growth come from "the blessing of God."[8] So, readers, my prayer is that you will live under that divine blessing.

The birth of a new baby is a wonderful event. Congratulations!

The birth of a new life in Christ is an eternal event. Hallelujah! *Born once, die twice. Born twice, die once.*

Now "grow in the grace and knowledge of our Lord and Savior Jesus Christ" (2 Peter 3:18).

Acknowledgments

For this book and the series of which it is a part, we owe even more thanks than usual to our editor at Viking, Brian Tart. It was Brian who saw the short meditation on death that Tim preached at the funeral of Terry Hall, Kathy's sister. He proposed that we turn it not only into one but three short books on birth, marriage, and death. We also thank our many friends in South Carolina who made it possible to write this and the companion books while at Folly Beach last summer.

Notes

First Birth

1. Derek Kidner, *Psalms 73–150: An Introduction and Commentary*, vol. 16, Tyndale Old Testament Commentaries (Downers Grove, IL: InterVarsity Press, 1975), 502–3.
2. Christy Raj has done some interesting work on gender in C. S. Lewis's Space trilogy, which you can access here: *withhandsopen.com*. I recommend all her posts, as well as a careful reading of *Out of the Silent Planet*, *Perelandra*, and *That Hideous Strength* for some of the most challenging and helpful reflections on masculinity/male and femininity/female ever written.
3. Jennifer Senior, *All Joy and No Fun: The Paradox of Modern Parenthood* (New York: HarperCollins, 2014), 43.
4. Senior, *All Joy and No Fun*, 44.
5. Senior, *All Joy and No Fun*, 8.
6. C. S. Lewis, *Prince Caspian* (New York: Macmillan, 1951), 182.

7. The majority of Christian churches in the world—Eastern Orthodox, Roman Catholic, Anglican, Lutheran, Presbyterian, and Reformed Methodist—practice infant baptism, but of course there are hundreds of millions of Christians who do not, who only baptize persons who are old enough to make a conscious profession of faith. We will not here try to make a case for infant baptism. Rather, we believe nearly all Christians will understand and practice, in one form or another, the basic spiritual move of both Israelite circumcision and Christian infant baptism—the move of offering your child to God, bringing them into the community of faith, and praying for and expecting his grace to come into your family for the task of parenting.

8. There are several versions of these questions on-line. They have obviously been altered for use in different churches, and it is not possible to tell which ones are the most original. I've given a representation of the slightly different forms.

9. Kim Tingley, "What Can Brain Scans Tell Us About Sex?," *New York Times Magazine*, September 18, 2019.

10. See James D. Hunter, *The Death of Character* (New York: Basic Books, 2001).

11. See Hunter, *The Death of Character*, Part Three: Unintended Consequences, 153–227. "There is a body of evidence that shows that moral education has its most enduring effects on young people when they inhabit a social world that coherently incarnates a moral [cosmology] defined by a clear and intelligible understanding of public and private good . . . where the school, youth organizations, and the larger community share a moral culture that is integrated and mutually reinforcing. . . . Needless to say, communities with this level of social and cultural integration and stability are scarce in America today" (155).

12. Alasdair MacIntyre, *After Virtue: A Study in Moral Theory* (South Bend, IN: University of Notre Dame Press, 2007).

13. These two views are well laid out in Kenneth Keniston and the Carnegie Council on Children, *All Our Children: The American Family Under Pressure* (New York: Houghton-Mifflin Harcourt Press, 1978).

14. Timothy Keller and Kathy Keller, *God's Wisdom for Navigating Life* (New York: Viking, 2016), 285.

Second Birth

1. It's important to consider that while the term "kingdom of God" is used constantly in the Synoptic Gospels of Matthew, Mark, and Luke, the Gospel writer John almost never uses the term. This is the only place, outside of a fleeting reference near the end of the book, where he mentions the term at all. This means the new birth in the New Testament is closely tied to the concept of God's kingdom.

2. "The term *hē palingenesia*, 'the rebirth' . . . [is] a term which is more typical of Stoic philosophy than of Jewish writers, but which aptly sums up the [Old Testament] eschatological hope of 'new heavens and a new earth' (Isaiah 65:17; 66:22, etc.). . . . In Stoic thought παλιγγενεσία was the term for the cyclical rebirth of the world as it rose from the ashes of its periodic conflagration." R. T. France, *The Gospel of Matthew*, New International Commentary on the New Testament (Grand Rapids, MI: William B. Eerdmans Publishing Co., 2007), 742–43.

3. This section is heavily dependent on Archibald Alexander, *Thoughts on Religious Experience*

(Edinburgh, Scotland: Banner of Truth Trust, 1967), 21–31.

4. Alexander, *Thoughts on Religious Experience*, 64.

5. New American Standard Bible.

6. Larry Hurtado, *Destroyer of the Gods* (Waco, TX: Baylor University Press, 2016), 93–94.

7. New American Standard Bible. The word "converted" is used here in the KJV and NASB translations. Other translations say merely we must "turn," but the Greek word *straphete* means a complete revolution from going one direction and turning to go in another direction. Jesus says that this turning means that spiritually we "become like children"—humbly trusting. This is why Bible scholar Leon Morris writes: "In this context it [the word *straphete*] will signify a change of direction of the whole life, a conversion." Leon Morris, *The Gospel According to Matthew*, Pillar New Testament Commentary (Grand Rapids, MI: William B. Eerdmans Publishing Co., 1992), 459.

8. Martin Luther, "Preface to Latin Writings," in *Luther's Works*, vol. 34 (St. Louis: Concordia, 1972), 336–37.

9. "'Hour' (*hōra*) constantly refers to his death on the cross and the exaltation bound up with it

(7:30; 8:20; 12:23, 27; 13:1; 17:1), or the consequences deriving from it (5:28–29), so it would be unnatural to take it in any other way here." D. A. Carson, *The Gospel According to John* (Leicester, England; Grand Rapids, MI: Inter-Varsity Press; W. B. Eerdmans, 1991), 171.

Growing in Grace

1. John Newton, *The Works of John Newton*, vol. 1 (Edinburgh, Scotland: Banner of Truth Trust, 1985), 197–217. The letters we are examining are the first three—"Grace in the Blade," "Grace in the Ear," and "The Full Corn in the Ear." As can be seen even by the titles of the three letters, Newton uses a number of images to describe what he calls A, B, and C Christians. I am here using only the metaphor of child, adolescent, and adult.
2. Newton, *The Works of John Newton*, vol. 1, 203.
3. Newton, *The Works of John Newton*, vol. 1, "On Grace in the Full Corn," 211.
4. Archibald Alexander, *Thoughts on Religious Experience* (Edinburgh, Scotland: Banner of Truth Trust, 1967), 159. Alexander adds that some

people go to such legalistic lengths to exercise self-control that "some do hesitate about taking their daily food" (159).

5. *William Cowper's Olney Hymns* (Minneapolis, MN: Curiosmith, 2017).

6. Alexander, *Thoughts on Religious Experience*, 160.

7. C. S. Lewis, *Mere Christianity* (New York: Macmillan, 1960).

8. "The soil enjoys the benefit of *rain* frequently showered upon it for its enrichment and fertility, so that it in turn may by its fruitfulness be of benefit to others. In fulfilling this function it is blessed of God. Spiritual productiveness is a manifestation of the operation of divine grace; for it is God who sends the rain of his mercy upon the soil of human lives, and who also as the husbandman tends his vineyard (Jn. 15:1) and gives the increase (1 Cor. 3:6f.)." Philip Edgcumbe Hughes, *A Commentary on the Epistle to the Hebrews* (Grand Rapids, MI: William B. Eerdmans Publishing Co., 1977), 222.

ALSO AVAILABLE

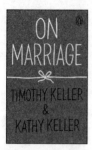

ON MARRIAGE

On Marriage is the perfect gift for anyone thinking about marriage. With wisdom, joy, and compassion, Timothy Keller and his wife, Kathy, teach us to understand marriage through the lens of the Bible, God's "owner's manual" for your life.

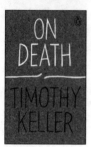

ON DEATH

In a culture that largely avoids thinking about the inevitability of death, Timothy Keller celebrates the Christian resources of hope in the face of death. Slim and compelling, *On Death* gives us the tools to understand God's triumph over death through the work of Jesus.